edexcel
advancing learning, changing lives

Edexcel

Functional Skills

English

Written by Clare C...

Consultants: Jen Gr...

Level

A PEARSON COMPANY

Heinemann is an imprint of Pearson Education Limited, a company incorporated in England and Wales, having its registered office at Edinburgh Gate, Harlow, Essex, CM20 2JE. Registered company number: 872828

www.pearsonschoolsandfecolleges.co.uk

Heinemann is a registered trademark of Pearson Education Limited

Text © Pearson Education Limited, 2010

First published 2010

12
10 9 8 7 6 5 4

British Library Cataloguing in Publication Data
A catalogue record for this book is available from the British Library.

ISBN 978 1 846 90880 4

Produced by Pearson Education Ltd, 2010
Typeset by Kamae Design
Original illustrations © Pearson Education, 2010
Cover design by Pete Stratton
Picture research by Caitlin Swain
Cover photo © Shutterstock images
Printed in Malaysia, CTP-KHL

Acknowledgements

The author and publisher would like to thank the following individuals and organisations for permission to reproduce photographs:

Cover © Norma Cornes/Shutterstock; P6–7 © Willie B. Thomas/iStockphoto; PP14–15 © Ruth Black/Shutterstock; PP14–15 © Ruth Black/Shutterstock; P16 © Miodrag Gajic/iStockphoto; P17 © Fuse/Getty Images; P18 Stephen Aaron Rees/Shutterstock; P19 © Cotswold Wildlife Park; PP20–21 © vinspired; P23 © Tall Stories; P27 © SunLu4ik/Shutterstock; P30 © DISNEY INCE 001-01/ MOVIESTORE COLLECTION LTD; P31 © Photolibrary; P34 © Andrew Butterton / Alamy; PP44–45 © Beau Lark/Corbis; P46 © Peter Titmuss / Alamy; P47 © Carlos Martinez/iStockphoto; P48 © Golden Pixels LLC/Shutterstock; P50 © Yellow Dog Productions/Getty Images; P51 © National Eczema Society; P51 © Chris Schmidt/iStockphoto; PP58–59 © Arieliona/Shutterstock; P63 © Chloe Parker / Alamy; P64 © Rich Legg/iStockphoto; P66 © Andrew Holbrooke/Corbis; P67 © Jupiterimages/Getty Images; P68 © Mick Sinclair / Alamy; P70 © Pearson Education Ltd/Steve Shott; P72 © Tim Graham/Getty Images; P74 (B) © Yuri Arcurs/Shutterstock; P74 (T) © Pali Rao/iStockphoto; P76 © UpperCut Images / Alamy; P78 © Agnieszka Kirinicjanow/iStockphoto; P80 (inset) © Anthony Lee/Getty Images; P80 © ampFotoStudio/Shutterstock; P82 © MBI / Alamy; P85 © Getty Images; P86 (inset) © MARKA / Alamy; P86 © MARKA / Alamy; P87 © Rex Features; P88 (L) © Anne Frank House, Amsterdam/Getty Images; P88 (R) © Getty Images; P91 © spinout/iStockphoto; P92 © Image Source / Alamy; P93 © Quicksnap Photo/Shutterstock; P94 © Photolibrary; P95 © Monkey Business Images/Shutterstock; P96 © Cynthia Farmer/Shutterstock; P99 © Corbis; P100 © Fiona Hanson/PA Archive/Press Association Images; P110 © Jim Wileman / Alamy; P112 © Andrey Shadrin/Shutterstock; P113 © Pearson Education Ltd/Jules Selmes; P114 © Yuri Arcurs/Shutterstock.

The author and publisher would like to thank the following individuals and organisations for permission to reproduce copyright material:

P9 THINK! poster. Published by the Department for Transport © Crown Copyright September 2005. Crown Copyright material is reproduced by the permission of the Controller of HMSO and Queen's Printer for Scotland; P11 innocent smoothie label. Reproduced by permission of innocent; P15 Lola's Kitchen Menu. Reproduced by permission of Lola's Kitchen Ltd. (www.lolas-kitchen.co.uk); P17 '18th Birthday or 21st Birthday – Which Is Larger?' article. Reproduced by permission of Your 18th (www.your18th.co.uk); P19 'Chameleon article'. Reproduced by kind permission of Oxford Journal/Ric Sumner; P21 'About the bigvbus' article. Reproduced by permission of vinspired (vinspired.com); P23 'CARE International London to Paris Cycle Challenge 2010' article. Reproduced by kind permission of www.tallstories.co.uk; P25 Crisis Christmas leaflet. Reproduced by kind permission of Crisis (www.crisis.org.uk); P29 'Girls Can Have Fun Too…' leaflet. Reproduced by kind permission of Surrey Cricket; P30 Information in Table A adapted from www.lovefilm.com. Reproduced by permission of LOVEFiLM.com; P32 'The eatwell plate'. Published by the Food Standards Agency © Crown Copyright 2007. Crown Copyright material is reproduced by the permission of the Controller of HMSO and Queen's Printer for Scotland; P33 charts reproduced by kind permission of Math League Press; P34 'Sorry you were out card', Royal Mail Cruciform (Standard) © and Trade Marks of Royal Mail Group Ltd. Reproduced by kind permission of Royal Mail Group Ltd. All rights reserved; P35 NSPCC/Clothes Aid collection bag. Reproduced by kind permission of NSPCC (www.nspcc.org.uk) and Clothes Aid (www.clothesaid.co.uk); P38 text from Crimestoppers website. Reproduced by kind permission of Crimestoppers (www.crimestoppers-uk.org); P51 Music in Hospitals text and logo. Reproduced with kind permission of Music in Hospitals (www.musicinhospitals.org.uk); National Eczema Society text and logo. Reproduced with kind permission of the National Eczema Society (www.eczema.org); Positive About Youth text and logo. Reproduced with kind permission of UK Youth (www.ukyouth.org).

Every effort has been made to contact copyright holders of material reproduced in this book. Any omissions will be rectified in subsequent printings if notice is given to the publishers.

We would like to thank the students and teachers of Thames Christian College for their invaluable help in the development and trialling of this course.

Websites
The websites used in this book were correct and up to date at the time of publication. It is essential for tutors to preview each website before using it in class so as to ensure that the URL is still accurate, relevant and appropriate. We suggest that tutors bookmark useful websites and consider enabling students to access them through the school/college intranet.

Contents

Introduction

Welcome to Edexcel Functional Skills English. This course aims to ensure that you are confident and capable when using the skills of speaking, listening, reading and writing.

Functional Skills English will equip you to communicate effectively, adapting to a range of audiences and contexts. We've worked hard to plan the course content to make sure you are fully prepared for your Functional Skills English assessments.

We hope you find the materials useful and wish you success in achieving a good Level 1 Pass.

Clare Constant,
Head of English
and Literacy

Keith Washington,
Chief Examiner
(pilot scheme)

How is this book structured?

This book is divided into three learning sections:

▶ Reading
▶ Speaking, listening and communication
▶ Writing.

These correspond to the three areas you will be assessed on for Functional Skills English.

Each section is broken down into lessons. Each lesson opens with its own learning objectives so that you are clear about the skills you are focusing on. You will then be given text and activities to help you learn, develop and practise those skills. Before you begin each lesson, think about how confident you are in the skills being covered. Then review your learning at the end. If you need to, set yourself a target for further improvement.

Assessment information and practice

At the end of each unit you will be given examples of the kinds of questions and activities you will meet in the assessments. For each, you will be given guidance from the examiner on what is expected. Have a go at completing the questions and activities, then assess how well you have done by comparing your work to the 'pass' and 'fail' sample answers provided. For each answer, the examiner explains what has been done well and what could be improved.

At the end of the book you will find a complete assessment practice section. Make sure you are clear about what is expected by reading 'How you will be assessed' and 'Top tips for success' on pages 113–117 before you attempt the practice papers and tasks.

ResultsPlus

These features combine expert advice and guidance from examiners to show you how to achieve better results.

Top tip
These provide guidance on how to improve your results.

ResultsPlus
Top tip

Key words in the question can help you decide which information in the text you need for your answer. Highlighting the key words in the question can help you to stay focused.

Self-assessment
These help you to think about what you can do well and what needs further improvement.

ResultsPlus
Self-assessment

For each unit of work, you will be given learning objectives. Read these carefully before you start and work out how confident you feel about your skills in that area. At the end of each unit, think about how your skills have improved and what still needs further practice.

Watch out!
These warn you about common mistakes that students often make so that you can avoid them!

ResultsPlus
Watch out!

You need to use a range of reading skills to find information in a table. Scanning the layout should help you find where to look, but then you must examine the details closely to find exactly what you need.

Maximise your marks
These pages show examples of student work that is typical of what might be produced by students whose overall performance was at a Level 1 'pass' or 'fail'. They are taken from real students' work. The examiner has commented on the work, showing what is done well and what could be improved. The examples and comments should help you to understand what is required to achieve a Level 1 pass.

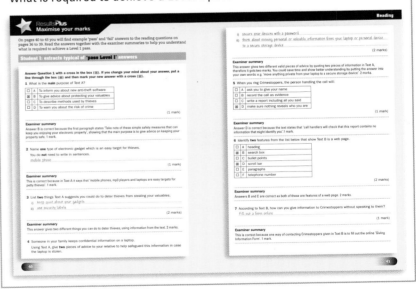

Introduction to reading

The texts and activities in this section of the book will help you to develop your skills in reading and understanding texts. You will practise:

- identifying the purposes of texts
- reading and understanding the main points and details in texts
- finding information in texts
- considering how to respond to texts.

At the end of the section you will find a short reading test. This will help you to practise and assess your reading skills in the kinds of questions you will meet in the test. There are also sample answers at pass and fail levels, with comments from the examiner. For a full practice test, see pages 118 to 123.

ResultsPlus
Self-assessment

For each unit of work, you will be given learning objectives. Read these carefully before you start, and work out how confident you feel about your skills in that area. At the end of each unit, think about how your skills have improved. What still needs further practice?

Your assessment

You will be assessed in one 45-minute test. You will be asked to read two texts about the same theme or topic, and answer questions about them. The questions will include multiple choice and short and longer responses. For more information on how you will be assessed, see page 112.

This table shows you the 'standards', or assessment objectives, that your reading will be assessed against.

Level 1 Skill standard for reading: *Read and understand a range of straightforward texts*
Identify the main points and ideas and how they are presented in a variety of texts
Read and understand texts in detail
Utilise information contained in texts
Identify suitable responses to texts

This lesson will help you to:
▶ understand what kind of text you are reading
▶ find the information you need in a text

Use what you already know about texts to help you understand a new one. Ask yourself:

▶ What **features** is the text made up of?

   headings   columns of words   paragraphs   addresses

▶ What **form** of text has those features?

   a newspaper article   a leaflet   a letter

▶ What **information** or **ideas** are given in the text?

   Use the features to help you find out.

Activity 1

1 Look at the outlines of Texts A and B below.

2 Use the features to work out what form of text each one is.

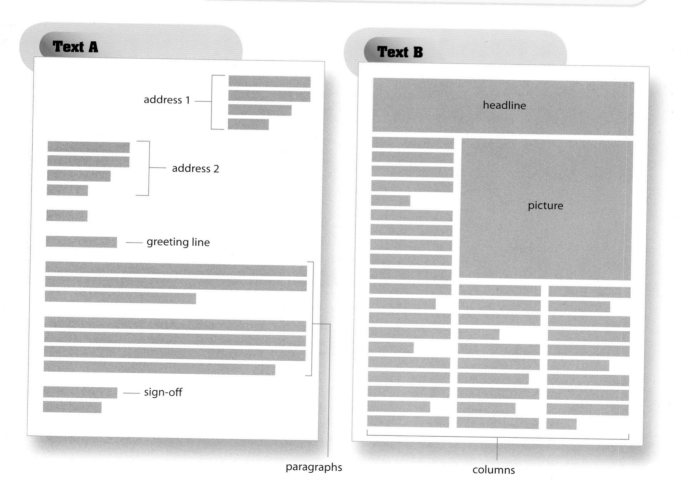

Text A

address 1

address 2

greeting line

sign-off

paragraphs

Text B

headline

picture

columns

Activity 2

1 Look at Text C below.

2 What are the features of the text? Choose from the ideas in the box below.

| paragraphs | charts | lists | headings | greetings | slogan | image |

3 a What is the form of the text? Choose from the options in the box below.

| letter | product packaging | poster | briefing note |

b Give reasons for your answer, explaining what features you can see that tell you what form the text is in.

Text C

55 teenagers a week wish they'd given the road their full attention.

THINK!

Results Plus
Top tip

Look first at features in the text, such as headings, addresses, lists and images, which tell you what kind of text it is. Then read the question before you read the whole text. This helps you to know what you are looking for when you read the text.

Activity 3

1 Look at Texts D to F.

2 What are the features of each text? Choose from the ideas in the box below.

| paragraphs | charts | lists | headings | greetings | slogan | image |

3 **a** What is the form of each text? Choose from the options in the box below.

| letter | product packaging | poster | briefing note |

b Give reasons for your answer, explaining what features you can see that tell you what form the text is in.

4 Use the texts to answer the questions below. Use what you know about the features of the texts to help you.
   a Chang wants to find out about learning online. Which text should he read?
   b Pia wants to know how much fat is in her drink. Which part of Text E should she read?

Text D

How can we make more effective use of ICT to aid students' learning?

Introduction

Students were asked to suggest ways in which ICT could be used to make learning more effective.

Findings

- Students suggested spending money on new software, mobile phones and visualisers.
- Free improvements suggested were: creating wiki pages; writing blogs; using forums, debating tools and chat rooms.

Recommendations

- The ICT and English departments should work together to look into the free options first.

Text E

3 GOOD REASONS TO DRINK THIS SMOOTHIE

1. THERE ARE 2 OF YOUR 5 A DAY IN EVERY BOTTLE
2. IT PROVIDES 14% OF YOUR GDA OF FIBRE
3. IT GIVES YOU THE GOODNESS OF 6 DIFFERENT TYPES OF FRUIT

PLEASE KEEP ME COLD
This product must be kept refrigerated 0-5°C before and after opening. Once opened consume within 2 days. For use-by date see cap. Gently pasteurised, just like milk. Shake it up baby.

AN INNOCENT SMOOTHIE IS A BLEND OF CRUSHED FRUIT & PURE JUICES

5 038862 320108

Ingredients
5 crushed strawberries (31%),
½ a pressed apple,
0 antimacassars*,
½ a mashed banana (23%),
a dash of squeezed orange,
5 pressed red & white grapes
and a squeeze of lime juice.

Nutritional info (per 100ml)
Energy	245kJ (58kcal)
Protein	0.7g
Carbohydrate	13.1g
(of which sugars†)	12.2g
Fat	trace
(of which saturates)	trace
Fibre	1.3g
Sodium	1mg
Vitamin C	26mg
	(43% RDA per 100ml)

†sugars found naturally in the fruit

*or lace doilies.

250ml ℮

100202
FCXXX
XXXXX

2 of your 5 a day

innocent™
pure fruit smoothie
strawberries & bananas

So, if I have this smoothie just before midnight, does it count towards my 5 a day for today or tomorrow?

It depends if you have your pyjamas on or not.

Bored of the iPad already? Pop round to Fruit Towers, 1 Goldhawk Estate, London W6 0BA, e-mail hello@innocentdrinks.com or call the banana phone on 020 8600 3993 (UK) or 01 664 4100 (ROI).

This bottle is made from 100% recycled plastic. Please recycle it so we can make more.

TM = Tricky Midnight

Text F

Dear Homeowner

I'm cleaning your neighbour's gutters and windows over the next few days. If you would like any of yours cleaned as well, please call me for a free estimate on 07672 398274.

5

Best regards
Charlie Harris
www.chmaintenance.com

This lesson will help you to:
▶ work out what a text is about and what its purpose is

Before using a text to find information, work out what it is about and what the writer is trying to do. This is the purpose of the text. To do this:

▶ Carefully look at every part of the text.

▶ Keep asking yourself: What is this about? Why has it been written? For example:

It's an advert persuading people to rent films from LOVEFiLM.com.

Activity 1

1 Look at Text A below.

2 Which of these sentences best describes the main purpose of the text?
   A It's an advert that tells you that you can top up your phone from £5 to £100.
   B It instructs you to top up your phone at stores that have the green top-up logo.
   C It explains how to use an E Top-up card to top up the amount you can spend using your mobile phone.
   D It persuades readers to use pay as you go.

Text A

E Top-up card

You'll get an E Top-up card with your joining pack, and it's a piece of cake to use:
- Decide how much you want to top up – you can choose from £5 to £100, in £5 denominations.
5
- Take your E Top-up card along to any store with the green top-up logo.
- Hand your card over to the store assistant – they'll swipe it through their machine and take your payment.

ResultsPlus
Top tip

In multiple-choice questions all the answers *seem* possible but only one is right. Read each answer carefully to choose which is exactly right.

Activity 2

1 Look at Text B below.

2 What does the writer of the text want you to do?

Text B

Calling all f⊙⊙tballers!

Do you fancy a kick-around in the park after school or college?
Do you want to get fit and have fun at the same time?
Then come and play football!

We play every Wednesday at 5pm in Fairfield Park.
Boys and girls of all ages are welcome!

If you'd like to sign up for the team just call 01378 279386.

Activity 3

1 Look at Texts C and D below.

2 What does the writer of Text C want the reader to do?

3 What is the main purpose of Text D?

Text C

1
2
3
4
5
6
7
8

FILMVAULT

PART OF THE HOME ENTERTAINMENT BUYING GROUP

Selling your Collection?

As the U.K.'s LARGEST BUYER* of private/trade owned collections for more than 30 years now; we make it easy for you.

SIMPLY SEND YOUR LIST** of DVDs, CDs, Console games and/or Videos to us.

Our PROFESSIONAL VALUERS will determine its current worth and contact you promptly.

If you wish to sell to us we will arrange FREE secure collection and IMMEDIATE PAYMENT once checked in.

Your listing can be sent via our website: www.filmvault.co.uk
by e-mail: mail@filmvault.co.uk
by Post: FREEPOST FILM VAULT (NO STAMP OR POSTCODE NEEDED),
or Fax to: 01865 327 600
Any questions? Please call anytime on: 01865 739 600

* Currently buying on average 114 collections every day.
** We will only accept genuine and original items in an as new condition without fault, damage or defacement.

Text D

Welcome to Home Entertainment's online shop

We stock a huge selection of home entertainment products including DVDs, blu-rays, CDs, etc.

5 All items listed are original official release items sourced from the UK's leading wholesalers: they are not bootlegs, copies or foreign imports. The DVDs are supplied direct to you as we receive them from the wholesaler. The vast majority are sealed, but the odd few are not sealed. However, they are brand-new unplayed discs.

The DVDs listed are region 2 UK pal format. Please ensure you can watch/play this kind of film prior to purchase as refunds will not be given for incompatibility.

This lesson will help you to:
- ▶ use different ways of finding information in a text
- ▶ identify the key words in a task
- ▶ find the key words in a text

ResultsPlus
Top tip

Key words in the question can help you decide which information in the text you need for your answer. If there seems to be more than one possible correct answer after you have skimmed the text, use close reading to decide which one is right.

You don't always need to read every word of a text to find the information you need in it. Instead, you can:

- ▶ Decide what important words you need to search for – the **key words**.
- ▶ Then search for the key words in the text by moving your eyes quickly over the page. This is called scanning a text.

Activity 1

1 Imagine you want to order a pizza. You need to decide what toppings you like. These will be your key words. Then look for those words in the menu.

2 Read this list of possible key words.

> pepperoni   onion   red peppers   olives
> mozzarella cheese   three cheeses   minced beef
> spicy chilli   tomatoes   egg   cheese crust   plain

3 Decide which of these words you could look for on the menu if you:
- **a** Like meat on your pizza.
- **b** Like hot spices on your pizza.
- **c** Like cheese on your pizza.

Activity 2

1 Now imagine you want to buy a cupcake. Look at the words in the box below.

> vanilla   peanut butter   chocolate   lemon   coffee
> banana   coconut   strawberry   chocolate milk

2 Which of these words could you search for if you want fruit on your cake?

3 Now list the words that tell you that a cupcake contains nuts.

Activity 3

1 Use Text A opposite for this activity. It is the cupcake menu for Lola's Kitchen.

2 Find two cupcakes decorated with a ring.

3 Now list a cupcake you could order for people who:
- **a** Like chocolate and sprinkles.
- **b** Like vanilla but not chocolate.
- **c** Want a ring on their cake but don't like fruit flavours.

Lola's Kitchen Menu

 vanilla — classic, fluffy, pure vanilla bean cupcake with vanilla buttercream icing and a signature ring

 chocolate — rich chocolate cupcake with chocolate buttercream icing and a signature ring

van milk chocolate — vanilla cupcake with fudgy milk chocolate icing and milk chocolate sprinkles

banana — moist, real banana cupcake with cream cheese icing and a signature ring

lemon — delectably light, fresh, lemon zest cupcake with lemon icing and a signature ring

4 Reading closely for detailed understanding

ResultsPlus
Watch out!

Marks are often lost through failing to read the question carefully and therefore not understanding what you are being asked to do. Read the text closely and answer each part of the question fully.

Close reading is reading a text carefully to gain a detailed understanding.

▶ First, work out what the text is about and what kind of text it is.

▶ Make sure you are clear about what information you want to find in it.

▶ Then scan to find the parts of the text you need to close read for that information.

▶ Read carefully every word in those parts. At the end of each sentence, stop and ask yourself: What did it tell me?

▶ If you don't understand a word or detail, read the whole sentence again and try to work it out.

Activity 1

1 Use Text A opposite for this activity. It is taken from the celebrations website 'Your18th.co.uk'

2 Scan the text. Decide which lines you need to read carefully to find the following pieces of information.
   a Reasons why reaching 21 used to be more important than reaching 18.
   b The difference between US and UK laws regarding being 21.
   c The minimum age at which Indian people can legally marry.
   d Three reasons why the author thinks reaching 18 is more significant than reaching 21.

3 Two students are discussing the text. They have misunderstood four points. Close read the script of their discussion below, then close read Text A to correct their mistakes.

> In the USA you can only vote once you are 18 because it's such a big responsibility, but in India you have to be 21 to marry if you are female.

> In the UK you have to be 21 to vote and marry. But you can gamble, drink and smoke at 16.

> Most teenagers think celebrating their 18th is a big deal, but people don't want to look forward to partying any more when they reach 21. They're too busy thinking about jobs and mortgages.

Text A

◄ ► + 18 http://www.your18th.co.uk/blog.html

YOUR 18th

Welcome to Your 18th! - 18th birthday ideas, 18th birthday gifts, 18th birthday celebrations and 18th birthday experiences!

18th Birthday or 21st Birthday – Which Is Larger?

Years ago a 21st was more significant as it was the age that gave you the full window of opportunity. You were considered an adult at 21 as you were able to vote and get a mortgage. These days in the UK you can do everything at 18
5   years of age, such as drinking, voting, gambling and buying cigarettes. However in the USA you still need to be 21 to legally do these things.

The only thing that you're allowed to do at 21 that you're not allowed to do at 18 is enter certain nightclubs that hold a policy encouraging the older generation to enter or keep teenagers out! In countries such as India, 21 is the minimum age
10   for a male to be officially permitted to marry. Similarly, the minimum age for girls is 18 years.

After asking many teenagers, the general consensus was that the 18th was the big birthday and was most important. I found this rather interesting as many 19–20-year-olds tend to think this way about being 21.

15   Overall I believe the 18th birthday is the larger of the two. 21st birthdays should still be considered as special birthdays, though. They are more a reality check and final throw into the real world. Throughout your twenties you will encounter anything from jobs and loans to mortgages and children: 21 is your real chance to celebrate adulthood and put your youth years behind you.

5 Identifying the main point in a paragraph

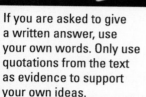

The main point in a paragraph is the big idea in it. To work out what it is:

▶ Look at the whole text, including the headings, to work out what it is about overall.

▶ Then read a paragraph carefully and ask yourself: What big idea is this paragraph about?

Activity 1

1 Use Text A below for this activity.

2 Look at the whole text and work out what it is about overall.

3 Read the first paragraph. Which of these statements about Welsh love spoons is true?
   A They are given to men by women.
   B They are given to friends and family.
   C They are carved by men for the girls they wish to marry.
   D They are a new idea.

4 Read the second paragraph. What tradition does it describe?

Text A

Welsh Wedding Traditions

The Welsh Love Spoon

The carving of a wooden love spoon is a courting tradition in Wales that has been in practice for many years. In order to express his intention of
5 marriage a man carves various symbols, such as hearts, bells or keys, into a wooden spoon. He then gives the spoon to the girl he wishes to marry.

Kidnapping of the Bride

Another marriage custom in Wales is for the bride's family to 'kidnap' her just before the wedding ceremony. The groom and his family must follow
10 in hot pursuit to rescue her. If the groom doesn't get to her first, it is said that whoever rescues the bride-to-be will marry someone within a year.

Activity 2

1 Use Text B below for this activity.

2 Which of the statements below are main points in the text?
   A The baby chameleons only measure a couple of inches.
   B Four baby chameleons have been born at Cotswold Wildlife Park.
   C One of the chameleons is called Olive.
   D Male chameleons can grow up to two feet in length.

3 In what order are these main points made in the text?
   A The chameleons have flattened bodies that are meant to look like leaves.
   B The species is normally found in Saudi Arabia, the United Arab Emirates and Yemen.
   C It is the first time this species has been successfully bred at Cotswold Wildlife Park.

Text B

Staff at Cotswold Wildlife Park have welcomed four tiny new additions to the fold in the new Reptile and Amphibian nursery.

Baby Yemen chameleons Olive, Emerald, Sage and Moss were all born between July 9 and 19, measuring little more than a couple of inches in length. It is the first time the species of chameleon, also known as veiled chameleons, have been successfully bred at the Burford park in Oxfordshire.

Male chameleons can grow up to two feet in length, and the tree dwelling animals are usually found in mountainous regions of Saudi Arabia, the United Arab Emirates and Yemen. The chameleons have a flattened body meant to mimic a leaf and feet specially designed for grasping limbs and branches.

6 Understanding main points and ideas

To find and understand a text's main ideas, follow these steps:

▶ First, work out the main idea of the whole text. Look at all the features and ask yourself: What are the headings, pictures and captions showing me?

▶ Then look at each paragraph in turn and ask: What is *this* part of the text about?

Activity 1

1 Use Text A opposite for this activity.

2 What is the main idea of the whole text? Use the text's features to help you decide.

3 Now work out what different paragraphs are about and answer these questions.
   a Why is the bigvbus going on tour?
   b For what teams are volunteers needed?
   c What will visitors to the bigvbus be able to do there?
   d Read the paragraph headed 'Green credentials'. What is its main idea?

Text A

 **vinspired**

Explore vinspired

the**bigvbus**
driven by **vinspired**.com

Home   Photos   Videos   Tour Dates   Tour Blog   About the bus   Game

About the bigvbus

1   **Why a bigvbus**

Vinspired connects 16–25-year-olds with volunteering opportunities in England.
This summer, vinspired is hitting the road in the bigvbus. We'll be touring the
country and the summer's hottest festivals, inspiring the nation's 16–25-year-olds
to spend their time doing some good – and you can come with us.
We're recruiting teams of volunteers to join our event crew and film production
team at the likes of T4 on the Beach, Relentless Boardmasters and Leeds Festival.

2   **Find out about opportunities in your area**

Whether you're looking for experience to
get a job, or you're just looking for
something good to do this summer, sit back,
chill out under the awning and grill our staff.
Or watch films for inspiration.

3   **Make a short film in our high-tech
film studio and video edit suite**

Sign up to go to one of our film workshops
and learn how to professionally make films
in our state-of-the-art film studio, which
has green screen technology so you can
change the background. Then upload it to
our site – there's free internet access.

4   **Access for all**

There's a ramp for the
ground floor and a lift
providing wheelchair
access to the top deck.

5   **Green credentials**

We've installed low-voltage LED lighting,
we're fully compliant with LEZ legislation
to meet low-exhaust emissions targets
and the engine can run on biodiesel.

This lesson will help you to:
▶ identify details in a text

ResultsPlus
Top tip

Make sure your answer gives exactly the details asked for by the question. You will not get full marks unless your answer is precise and sufficiently detailed.

To find a specific detail in a text, follow these steps:

▶ Decide what you need to find out.

▶ Look over the text to work out where that information is likely to be.

▶ Scan that part of the text for key words to find the sentence or line you need.

▶ Read that part of the text carefully, searching for the detail you want.

Activity 1

1 Use Text A opposite for this activity. It is the first part of a web page about a London to Paris cycle challenge.

2 You want to find out the least amount of sponsorship money you can raise.
  a Look over the text. Where is the information about sponsorship?
  b Read it carefully for the detail you need and write it down.

3 You want to find out how far you will travel on day 1.
  a Look over the text. Where is the information about day 1?
  b Read it carefully for the detail you need and write it down.

4 Now use the same steps to find out where will you eat your three meals on day 2.

5 Now use the same steps to fill in the details about day 2 on this postcard.

Hi everyone

We had to cycle for _____ on the second day but at least we got to _____ on the ferry from _____ first. Two of the wonderful things we saw were _____ and _____. We stayed the night in Bernay, which has a famous _____ abbey.

Can't wait to tell you more about it!

Text A

Tall Stories Charity Challenges

Charities | Corporates | Participants | Upcoming Events | Blog | About Us | Contact

CARE International London to Paris Cycle Challenge 2010

Charity: CARE International UK
Challenge: London to Paris Bike Ride
Dates: 01/07/2010 to 04/07/2010
Deposit: £100
5 Minimum Sponsorship: £1300
Grade: Moderate

Trip description
Cycle from London to Paris in three days. Conquer the North and South Downs
on your way through the beautiful English countryside to Portsmouth. Then cycle
10 through French vineyards and small villages to a 'triumphant' finish at the Arc de
Triomphe or the Eiffel Tower in Paris!

Day 1: London to Portsmouth
114km/71 miles 1200m Ascent
We meet early on Thursday morning in Twickenham. After a briefing and safety talk,
15 we will divide up into our different groups. Each of these groups has its own guide
and is made up of ten riders of a similar fitness and speed. Making our way out of
town we pass through Hampton Court. It is an area rich in history and fabulous to
pass through on a bike with the River Thames never far away. We continue on from
here along small country roads to our lunch spot in the heart of Surrey. As the roads
20 get smaller, we pass through the prettiest of villages, heading up and down the hills,
over the North Downs, to our tea break before we head off the South Downs and into
Portsmouth. Dinner and accommodation in a local hotel.

Day 2: Caen to Bernay
100km/63 miles 630m Ascent
25 We have a very early start to make the ferry departure at 07.00 from Portsmouth.
On board we relax, have breakfast, catch up on our sleep and before mid-day we
arrive in the village of Ouistreham, just north of Caen, in France. We have a short
briefing before we head off on the cycle path and into the French countryside with a
fabulous picnic lunch just a couple of hours away. As we pass tiny villages, bubbling
30 brooks, 'villes fleuries', farmhouses and fields of horses, we approach the end of our
day's cycling in the town of Bernay. The town has a long and well-known history as
shown by the Benedictine abbey, the medieval buildings and the remains of mills all
around. We spend the night in a wonderful local hotel and eat in a nearby restaurant.

Day 3: Bernay to Arc de Triomphe, Paris

This lesson will help you to:
▶ understand the main points and the details in a text

When you are searching a text for details, make sure you understand the text fully. Use the following strategies:

▶ Read each sentence of the text carefully. Then ask yourself: What did that tell me?

▶ At the end of each paragraph, stop and ask yourself: What did that tell me?

▶ If you don't understand a word, sentence or paragraph, read through that part of the text again, slowly and carefully. Use the sentences that come before and after it to help you work out what it means.

▶ Use any pictures, headings and captions to help you work out the meaning.

Activity 1

1 Use Text A opposite for this activity.

2 List three different facts about the Crisis Centre.

3 Identify two ways in which Crisis helps their guests.

4 Which of the following statements about the Crisis Centre is true?
   A The Crisis Centre only opens at Christmas.
   B Guests can live at the Crisis Centre permanently.
   C There are no computers available at the Crisis Centre.
   D Coming to the Crisis Centre gives people a chance to move on from being homeless.

Activity 2

1 Use Text A opposite for this activity.

2 Read two people's responses to the text, which are given in the speech bubbles below. Do you agree or disagree with them? Use details from Text A to give reasons for your views.

> Giving money to the Crisis Centre is a waste. It's cruel to give homeless people a taste of luxury and then send them back out on the streets.

> This charity really knows what homeless people need to be able to change.

ResultsPlus
Watch out!

When replying to a text, make sure you understand the main points before you start your reply.

Text A

Getting started

1 *"It was one of the only times in the year when I felt human. Crisis Christmas made me feel like a normal person again."*

2 We believe all of our guests have the potential to find a job and a permanent home, but they rarely get the chance to develop their skills and prove themselves.

3 At Crisis, we provide a range of services enabling people to brush up on their skills and develop new ones.

4 *£50 could enable two homeless people to learn new skills*

5 We also help people prepare to find and keep a job. Every year, these services move into our centres for Christmas. Help is on hand to help improve maths and literacy.

6 There's also a well-stocked library where guests can get lost in a good book.

7 Each centre has a well-equipped IT suite, so people can access computers. For many it's the first time they've ever used a computer and sent an email. It gives them the opportunity to get in touch and reunite with friends and family. They can also create their own CV, with a little help from our career advisors, so they're all set for job searching after Christmas.

8 *144 guests wrote CVs or job applications last Christmas*

9 Our guests also want somewhere to call home. We have housing advice services to help people find and keep accommodation in the new year. After their experience at Crisis Christmas, we want all of our guests to have the confidence and drive to make a real difference to their lives. This is just the first step. With support from people like you, we'll be there to help them throughout the year.

9 Identifying how texts are presented

This lesson will help you to:
- identify the different presentation features used in a text
- understand why they are used

ResultsPlus
Watch out!

It is not enough just to identify the presentation features used in a text. You have to be able to work out *why* they have been used.

Texts can use different presentation features such as headings, bullet points or paragraphs to present information. When you are given a new text:

- Skim the text to see how it is organised and what presentation features are used.

- Notice where a presentation feature is used and work out what that part of the text is telling you. Ask yourself: How does this feature help the writer to convey their ideas to their readers?

Activity 1

1 Use Texts A, B and C for this activity.

2 Look at the features of the three texts. Decide which one is:
- an advert
- a poster
- an email.

3 **a** Which of the texts has a heading? How does it help the reader to understand what the text is about?
   b Which text uses a reference directing the reader to another text? Why might this be useful for the reader?
   c Why has an image been included in Text B?
   d How does the chart in Text C help the reader to understand the information?

Text A

Hi Dave

Have you seen the snow glider on *The Gadget Show*? As far as I can tell it's a sledge that is like a helicopter on three skis. It can go across snow and ice at up to 130km per hour. How cool is that?!

5 Here's the link for you to take a look at it:

http://fwd.five.tv/gadgets/sports/mountain/snow-glider

Do you think we should look into stocking these ready for next winter?

Baz

Text B

Swooping through the snow at amazing speed...

This winter ... it could be you!

Text C

Snow Business

Businessmen Dave Stokes and 'Baz' Mohammed are looking to become the UK's number 1 stockists of snow gliders.

'We know winters are getting longer and we see more snow every year. Having a snow glider will be a fun, cheap and reliable way to travel when there is heavy snow, and great fun for the family at weekends,' said Baz.

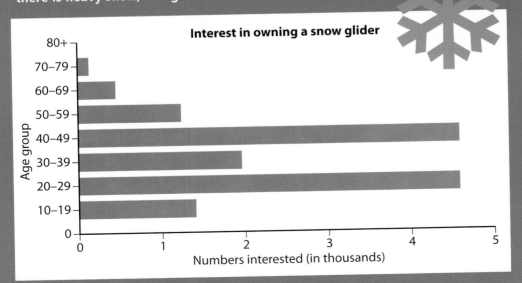

Interest in owning a snow glider

Age group (y-axis): 0, 10–19, 20–29, 30–39, 40–49, 50–59, 60–69, 70–79, 80+

Numbers interested (in thousands) (x-axis): 0, 1, 2, 3, 4, 5

This lesson will help you to:
▶ understand presentation features
▶ explain what effect they have on readers

Results**Plus**
Top tip

When you are asked to find the purpose of a text, think about who is likely to read it and if the reader is expected to do anything after reading it.

Writers often use presentation features to help them achieve their purpose. When you read a text:

▶ Identify which presentation features have been used, such as headings, pictures, blocks of text, different types of print and coloured backgrounds.

▶ Look at the whole page and ask yourself: What stands out most? Why? For example, pictures and brightly coloured print can stand out more than text and pale print.

▶ Then ask: Why does the writer want their audience to notice this feature? How does it help to achieve the text's purpose?

Activity 1

1 Use Text A opposite for this activity.

2 What is the main purpose of Text A?
   A It argues that teenage girls should play cricket.
   B It warns boys that girls are going to play cricket too, so there will be mixed teams in Kingston.
   C It informs readers in general that three cricket clubs are looking for girls to join their teams.
   D It persuades girls that in Kingston cricket is not just a boys' game, so girls can enjoy trying it out too.

3 a Read the table below. Find three more presentation features the writer has used in Text A.
   b Copy the table below and list your three extra features in column one.
   c Think about what each feature makes the reader notice in the text. Write your ideas in column two.
   d Try to work out how the features help to achieve the text's purpose. Write your ideas in column three.

Presentation feature	What does it make readers notice?	How does this help the text achieve its purpose?
1 Heading: large white print against a bright-red background.	The words in the heading make you think about who is having fun already – boys. This is saying girls don't have to be left out.	Red is a warm, energetic colour – it stands out and creates a feeling of fun and excitement. It can also be used as a warning. White makes you think of cricket whites. It's also a strong contrast with red.
2 Information bubble with jagged edge: white text against a red background.	It makes it clear to the reader that the scheme is important, as it's supported by high-profile sporting bodies such as Surrey Cricket.	It reinforces the fact that this is an important, official campaign to get girls interested in playing cricket.
3		
4		
5		

Text A

Girls Can Have Fun Too...

The scheme is supported by Surrey Cricket, Kingston School Sport Partnership and Active Kingston

Three clubs in the Royal Borough of Kingston are working together to provide cricket for girls of all ages and abilities.

The clubs involved in this scheme are:

Chessington CC
www.chessington.play-cricket.com
Tuesday Evening Coaching 6:30pm - 8:30pm

Worcester Park CC
www.wparkcc.co.uk
Tuesday Evening Coaching 6:30pm - 8:00pm

Malden Wanderers CC
www.maldenwanderers.play-cricket.com
Monday Evening Coaching 6:30pm - 8:00pm

Towards the end of each month the girls and coaches from each club will come together at one of the clubs for joint coaching and matches.

Don't miss out on this opportunity of giving cricket a go!

Please contact the relevant club for more information on how to get involved!

This lesson will help you to:
▶ find and use information presented in tables

ResultsPlus
Top tip

Use all your reading skills to find information in a table. Scan the layout to work out where to look, then look closely at the details to find what you need.

Information may be presented in tables containing words or numbers. To find information in a table:

▶ Read the headings of the columns and rows to find out how the information is organised.

▶ Search for the right row and column to use for what you need to find out.

▶ Move your finger along the row or column until you find the information.

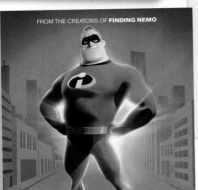

FROM THE CREATORS OF **FINDING NEMO**

Activity 1

1 Use Table A below for this activity. Imagine you are interested in famous films and have found the information in the table on the LOVEFiLM website.

2 Follow the steps listed above to find the answers to the following questions by searching in the table.
   a When was *Toy Story* released?
   b Who starred in *The Incredibles*?
   c Which film was rated ★★★★ by 70,628 members?
   d Which two films are rated certificate 15?
   e Which two films were released in 2001?

Table A

Title	Date released	Starring	Certificate	Member rating
Shrek	2001	Mike Myers, Eddie Murphy, Cameron Diaz, Jim Cummings	U	★★★★★ by 62,102 members
Finding Nemo	2003	Albert Brooks, Alexander Gould, Ellen DeGeneres, Willem Dafoe	U	★★★★★ by 70,628 members
Amélie	2001	Audrey Tautou, Mathieu Kassovitz, Yolande Moreau, Dominique Pinon	15	★★★★★ by 64,556 members
Monty Python's Life of Brian	1979	Graham Chapman, John Cleese, Terry Gilliam, Eric Idle	15	★★★★★ by 54,547 members
Toy Story	1995	Tom Hanks, Annie Potts, Tim Allen, Jim Varney	U	★★★★★ by 60,483 members
The Incredibles	2004	Craig T Nelson, Holly Hunter, Samuel L Jackson, Jason Lee	U	★★★★★ by 83,242 members

Activity 2

1 Use Table B below to find the answers to the following questions.

2 At what time does the first train leave Manchester Oxford Road?

3 At what time does the first train from Warrington Central arrive at Liverpool Lime Street?

4 How many trains stop at all stations?

Table B

Mondays to Saturdays

		NT	NT	NT	NT SO	NT SX	NT SX	NT A	TP	NT SX	NT SO	EM	NT	NT A	TP	NT	EM	NT	NT A	TP	NT
Manchester Airport	d	0434				0545		0641	0641			0705		0741	0741		0805		0841	0841	
Manchester Piccadilly	d	0449				0603		0658	0707			0734		0758	0807		0837		0901	0907	
Manchester Oxford Rd	d				0622	0627	0646	0701	0711			0737	0739	0803	0811	0815	0841	0844	0904	0911	0916
Birchwood	d				0649	0654	0704		0724				0804		0824	0840		0903		0924	0940
Warrington Central	d		0603	0637	0656	0701	0712a		0729	0735	0740	0753	0811		0829	0846	0857	0910		0929	0946
Liverpool Lime St	a	0532	0645	0720c	0740	0748		0749	0757	0818	0821	0831	0855	0859	0857	0924	0931	0953	0948	0957	1024

Activity 3

1 Use Table B above for this activity.

2 Read the three paragraphs below.

3 Use the table to find the best trains for Kerri, Ashley and Mo to catch.

Kerri

Kerri lives near Birchwood station. She has a haircut booked for 9.20 in a salon that is near to Liverpool Lime Street station. Which train should she catch to make sure she arrives at the salon on time?

Ashley

Ashley has a job interview near the station in Warrington at 9.00. Which train should he catch from Manchester Piccadilly to get there on time?

Mo

Mo is seeing his older brother off at Manchester Airport at 6.30. He needs to meet his friends at Birchwood station by 8.10am to walk to school. Which train should he take?

This lesson will help you to:
▶ find and use information presented in charts

Charts may be used to present information visually. This can make the information easier to find and understand. There may be a key that tells you what each area of the chart represents.

A pie chart shows information as 'slices' of a 'pie'. The bigger the slice, the higher the number.

A bar chart shows information as blocks of colour. The taller the block, the higher the number.

Activity 1

1 Use Chart A below for this activity.

2 Study the chart, which shows how much of different foods you should eat to stay healthy.

3 Which of the following statements is true, according to the chart?
   A You should eat roughly the same amount of non-dairy sources of protein as starchy foods.
   B You can have more food and drinks high in fat and/or sugar than non-dairy sources of protein.
   C Fruit and vegetables should make up more of your diet than milk and dairy foods.
   D You need to eat more milk and dairy foods than starchy foods.

Chart A

The eatwell plate

Food Standards Agency
eatwell.gov.uk

Use the eatwell plate to help you get the balance right. It shows how much of what you eat should come from each food group.

Fruit and vegetables

Bread, rice, potatoes, pasta and other starchy foods

Meat, fish, eggs, beans and other non-dairy sources of protein

Foods and drinks high in fat and/or sugar

Milk and dairy foods

Activity 2

1 Use Chart B below for this activity. The chart shows the different ingredients of a sausage and mushroom pizza. Each 'slice' of the 'pie' represents a different ingredient.

2 According to the chart, which of the following statements is true?
   A The largest topping ingredient on the pizza is tomato sauce.
   B The sausages make up the smallest amount of the pizza topping.
   C Mushrooms and sausages combined make up a quarter of the pizza topping.
   D Half of the pizza's weight comes from the crust.

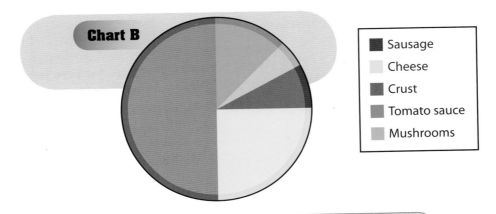

Chart B

Legend:
- Sausage
- Cheese
- Crust
- Tomato sauce
- Mushrooms

Activity 3

1 Use Chart C below for this activity.

2 A local café is thinking about producing fast food for students. Using the information from the chart, list two points about how popular different kinds of fast food are.

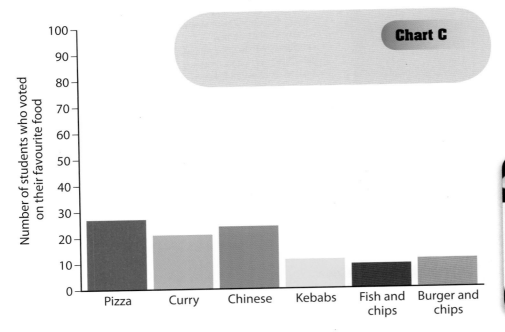

Chart C

Number of students who voted on their favourite food

y-axis: 0, 10, 20, 30, 40, 50, 60, 70, 80, 90, 100

x-axis: Pizza, Curry, Chinese, Kebabs, Fish and chips, Burger and chips

ResultsPlus
Watch out!

Only include information taken from the right text. You will gain no marks for information from other sources, even if it is correct.

This lesson will help you to:
▶ decide how to respond to a text

ResultsPlus
Top tip

Look closely at the question for information about how to respond. The number of marks for the question and the space given for your answer will give you clues about how much to write.

Most writers want their readers to respond to the text. To do this, you will need to:

▶ Work out the purpose of the text, such as if it is telling you how to do something or if it is selling you something.

▶ Look for instructions that tell you what you have to do.

▶ Plan the best way to respond. For example, if you need to find certain information, go through the text and underline or jot down the details you need.

Text A

As you requested your item has been left:

☐ In your 'Safeplace' on your property at:

☐ with your designated neighbour at:

☑ **Has been returned to the Royal Mail Delivery Office at:**

Royal Mail
Walton-On-Thames Delivery Office
73 Hersham Road
WALTON ON THAMES
KT12 1LN
Tel: 08456 112775
HOURS: MON-SAT: 0730 - 1300

You can:

Collect the item. Please leave ☐ hours before collecting. You'll need to bring this card and evidence of your identity such as a passport or bank card. If someone's collecting on your behalf, they'll need to provide proof of your identity.

Redelivery or Local Collect® services:
to arrange visit us online at **www.royalmail.com/redelivery**
or call the number above.
We can **Redeliver** to your address or to an alternative local address (unfortunately, we can't redeliver Special Delivery or Royal Mail Tracked items to an alternative address).
Or you can have your item taken to a local Post Office® branch for you to pick up using our **Local Collect®** service.*
*visit www.royalmail.com for prices

Please note we'll keep a Recorded item for 1 week, Royal Mail Tracked item for 2 weeks and all other items for 3 weeks before returning them to the sender.

If you are deaf or hard-of-hearing, and have access to a textphone please call 0845 600 0606

PT59 APR 09 Royal Mail is a trading name of Royal Mail Group Ltd. Registered in England and Wales. Registered number 4138203 Registered office 100 Victoria Embankment. LONDON EC4Y 0HQ

Activity 1

1 Use Text A above for this activity.

2 Where is your parcel now?

3 What do you have to do if you want to collect your parcel?

4 What do you have to do if you want your parcel to be redelivered?

Text B

NSPCC
Cruelty to children must stop. FULL STOP.

YOUR COLLECTION DAY IS:
THURSDAY

Help Clothes Aid support the NSPCC by giving good quality clothes, shoes and other textiles. No bric-a-brac or toys, please.

Clothes Aid drivers will be around to collect your clothing between **8am and 7pm**. Please leave your bags at the edge of your property in full view of the road.

Income raised by Clothes Aid wil help fund NSPCC projects and services throughout the UK, including ChildLine and the NSPCC Helpline. For more information about the NSPCC, please see **www.nspcc.org.uk**

If you cannot use this bag, please store it and use it next time we are collecting. **Thanks**

Help us raise funds for the NSPCC. Clothes Aid (Services) Ltd will donate at least £75 per tonne of clothes collected to the NSPCC registered charity number 216401 and SC037717 via the NSPCC Trading Company Ltd. Clothes Aid (Services) Ltd have guaranteed to donate a minimum of £525,000 plus VAT in a 12 month period.

For any queries about the collections, please call the
Clothes Aid Helpline: 08450 722780
Calls are charged at national rates
Office open: 9am–5pm Monday to Friday
www.clothesaid.co.uk
Unit 4NR Leroy House,
436 Essex Road, London N1 3QP

CL⊙THES**AID**

Activity 2

1 Use Text B above for this activity.

2 Which words tell you what the NSPCC wants you to do?

3 Imagine you have some old clothes you would like to give away. What three things do you have to do to make sure the NSPCC can make money from them?

Read Text A and answer the questions that follow.

Text A

Keep Your Electronic Valuables Safe

It's important to realise that luxuries such as mobile phones, MP3 players and laptops are easy targets for petty thieves. Follow these simple safety measures that can keep you enjoying your electronic property.

5 Never leave your possessions unsupervised for any length of time, no matter where you are. Keep them with you under all circumstances.

Although you may want to brag about your newest gadget, a potential thief may be listening. It's better to keep quiet and leave your electronics in your briefcase, your handbag or your pockets.

Consider applying security labels to your valuables. A thief is less likely to steal
10 electronic equipment if he or she has to risk being caught due to removing security labels.

Secure your devices with a password. This way, even if your belongings are stolen, the thief can't easily find any personal or valuable data.

If you are using your portable electronics in public and on the go, think about
15 moving personal or valuable information from your laptop or personal device to a secure storage device.

Finally, keep in mind that simply deleting data does not guarantee that it cannot be recovered if it falls into the wrong hands. If you want to completely delete information, use additional software designed to keep files confidential.

Answer Question 1 with a cross in the box (☒). If you change your mind about your answer, put a line through the box (☒) and then mark your new answer with a cross (☒).

1 What is the **main** purpose of Text A?

☐	A	To inform you about new anti-theft software
☐	B	To give advice about protecting your valuables
☐	C	To describe methods used by thieves
☐	D	To warn you about the risk of crime

(1 mark)

ResultsPlus
Top tip

Question 1 is an example of the kind of multiple choice question you will be asked. You need to choose the best of the four possible answers given. The writer may have had more than one aim in writing the text, but this question asks you to explain which you think was the main (most important) purpose. Test out all four answers carefully before you make up your mind – only one answer is correct, but more than one may appear to be right at first glance.

2 Name **one** type of electronic gadget which is an easy target for thieves.

You do **not** need to write in sentences.

.... (1 mark)

ResultsPlus
Top tip

For this question, you need to find the answer in Text A and write it down – there will be a space on the exam paper for your answer. Note that you do not need to write your answer in sentences, but make sure your answer gives all the information you need to answer the question. Your answer must be found in Text A – you will receive no marks for answers based on information from any other source, even if the information is true.

3 List **two** things Text A suggests you could do to deter thieves from stealing your valuables.

i) ....

ii) .... (2 marks)

ResultsPlus
Top tip

This question is also asking you to find information in the text. Read the question carefully – **two** methods are needed to obtain the two marks available.

4 Someone in your family keeps confidential information on a laptop.

Using Text A, give **two** pieces of advice to your relative to help safeguard this information in case the laptop is stolen.

i) ....

ii) .... (2 marks)

ResultsPlus
Top tip

This open response question tests how well you can use the information you have read in the text. Look for **two** different points and make sure each point is clearly stated using your own words.

Read Text B and answer the questions that follow.

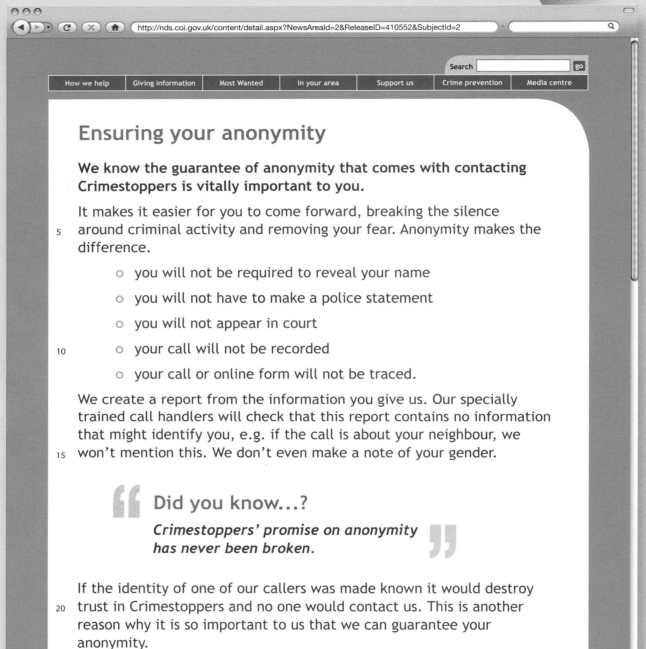

http://nds.coi.gov.uk/content/detail.aspx?NewsAreaId=2&ReleaseID=410552&SubjectId=2

Search [   ] go

| How we help | Giving information | Most Wanted | In your area | Support us | Crime prevention | Media centre |

Ensuring your anonymity

We know the guarantee of anonymity that comes with contacting Crimestoppers is vitally important to you.

It makes it easier for you to come forward, breaking the silence around criminal activity and removing your fear. Anonymity makes the difference.

- you will not be required to reveal your name
- you will not have to make a police statement
- you will not appear in court
- your call will not be recorded
- your call or online form will not be traced.

We create a report from the information you give us. Our specially trained call handlers will check that this report contains no information that might identify you, e.g. if the call is about your neighbour, we won't mention this. We don't even make a note of your gender.

" Did you know...?
Crimestoppers' promise on anonymity has never been broken. "

If the identity of one of our callers was made known it would destroy trust in Crimestoppers and no one would contact us. This is another reason why it is so important to us that we can guarantee your anonymity.

To give information anonymously to Crimestoppers now, call **0800 555 111** or fill out our anonymous online Giving Information Form.

Answer Question 5 with a cross in the box you think is correct (☒). If you change your mind about an answer, put a line through the box (☒) and then mark your new answer with a cross (☒).

5 When you ring Crimestoppers, the person handling the call will:

☐	A	ask you to give your name
☐	B	record the call as evidence
☐	C	write a report including all you said
☐	D	make sure nothing reveals who you are

(1 mark)

Answer Question 6 with a cross in the **two** boxes you think are correct ☒.

6 Identify **two** features from the list below that show Text B is a webpage.

☐	A	heading
☐	B	search box
☐	C	bullet points
☐	D	scroll bar
☐	E	paragraphs
☐	F	telephone number

(2 marks)

7 According to Text B, how can you give information to Crimestoppers without speaking to them?

....

(1 mark)

On pages 40 to 43 you will find example 'pass' and 'fail' answers to the reading questions on pages 36 to 39. Read the answers together with the examiner summaries to help you understand what is required to achieve a Level 1 pass.

Student 1: extracts typical of 'pass Level 1' answers

Answer Question 1 with a cross in the box (☒). If you change your mind about your answer, put a line through the box (☒) and then mark your new answer with a cross (☒).

1 What is the **main** purpose of Text A?

☐	A	To inform you about new anti-theft software
☒	B	To give advice about protecting your valuables
☐	C	To describe methods used by thieves
☐	D	To warn you about the risk of crime

(1 mark)

Examiner summary

Answer B is correct because the first paragraph states 'Take note of these simple safety measures that can keep you enjoying your electronic property', showing that the main purpose is to give advice on keeping your property safe. 1 mark.

2 Name **one** type of electronic gadget which is an easy target for thieves.

You do **not** need to write in sentences.

mobile phone

(1 mark)

Examiner summary

This is correct because in Text A it says that 'mobile phones, mp3 players and laptops are easy targets for petty thieves'. 1 mark.

3 List **two** things Text A suggests you could do to deter thieves from stealing your valuables.

i) keep quiet about your gadgets

ii) use security labels

(2 marks)

Examiner summary

This answer gives two different things you can do to deter thieves, using information from the text. 2 marks.

4 Someone in your family keeps confidential information on a laptop.

Using Text A, give **two** pieces of advice to your relative to help safeguard this information in case the laptop is stolen.

   i)   <u>secure your devices with a password</u> ....

   ii) <u>think about moving personal or valuable information from your laptop or personal device</u> ....

      <u>to a secure storage device</u> ....

(2 marks)

Examiner summary

This answer gives two different valid pieces of advice by quoting two pieces of information in Text A, therefore it gets two marks. You could save time and show better understanding by putting the answer into your own words: e.g. 'move anything private from your laptop to a secure storage device'. 2 marks.

5 When you ring Crimestoppers, the person handling the call will:

☐	A	ask you to give your name
☐	B	record the call as evidence
☐	C	write a report including all you said
☒	D	make sure nothing reveals who you are

(1 mark)

Examiner summary

Answer D is correct because the text states that 'call handlers will check that this report contains no information that might identify you'. 1 mark.

6 Identify **two** features from the list below that show Text B is a web page.

☐	A	heading
☒	B	search box
☐	C	bullet points
☒	D	scroll bar
☐	E	paragraphs
☐	F	telephone number

(2 marks)

Examiner summary

Answers B and D are correct as both of these are features of a web page. 2 marks.

7 According to Text B, how can you give information to Crimestoppers without speaking to them?

   <u>Fill out a form online</u> ....

(1 mark)

Examiner summary

This is correct because one way of contacting Crimestoppers given in Text B is to fill out the online 'Giving Information Form'. 1 mark.

Student 2: extracts typical of 'fail Level 1' answers

1 What is the **main** purpose of Text A?

☒	A	To inform you about new anti-theft software
☐	B	To give advice about protecting your valuables
☐	C	To describe methods used by thieves
☐	D	To warn you about the risk of crime

(1 mark)

Examiner summary

Answer A is incorrect because Text A does not mention 'new' software. Also, only the final paragraph concerns the use of software so this is not the main purpose. 0 marks.

2 Name **one** type of electronic gadget which is an easy target for thieves.

You do **not** need to write in sentences.

A Nintendo

(1 mark)

Examiner summary

This is incorrect because although a Nintendo is an electronic gadget, it is not mentioned in Text A. 0 marks.

3 List **two** things Text A suggests you could do to deter thieves from stealing your valuables.

i) Never leave your possessions unsupervised for any length of time.

ii) Keep them with you under all circumstances.

(2 marks)

Examiner summary

Although this answer does give relevant information taken from the text, the two answers are different ways of saying the same thing. Make sure you give two **different** actions to get the two marks. 1 mark.

4 Someone in your family keeps confidential information on a laptop.

Using Text A, give **two** pieces of advice to your relative to help safeguard this information in case the laptop is stolen.

i) leave your electronics in your briefcase, your handbag or your pockets.

ii) keep in mind that simply deleting data does not guarantee that.

(2 marks)

5 When you ring Crimestoppers, the person handling the call will:

☐	A	ask you to give your name
☐	B	record the call as evidence
☒	C	write a report including all you said
☐	D	make sure nothing reveals who you are

(1 mark)

6 Identify **two** features from the list below that show Text B is a web page.

☐	A	heading
☐	B	search box
☒	C	bullet points
☐	D	scroll bar
☒	E	paragraphs
☐	F	telephone number

(2 marks)

7 According to Text B, how can you give information to Crimestoppers without speaking to them?

ring 0800 555111 anonymously

(1 mark)

Introduction to speaking, listening and communication

The activities in this section of the book will help you to develop your skills in speaking, listening and communication in formal and informal discussions. You will practise:

- contributing to discussions in different ways
- responding to others in discussions
- presenting your information and points of view clearly
- using appropriate language.

At the end of the section you will find two speaking, listening and communication tasks. These will help you to practise and assess the skills you will need to use in the assessment. There is also guidance from the examiner. For a full practice assessment, see pages 124 to 125.

Self-assessment

For each unit of work, you will be given learning objectives. Read these carefully before you start, and work out how confident you feel about your skills in that area. At the end of each unit, think about how your skills have improved. What still needs further practice?

Your assessment

You will be assessed in your school or college, taking part in two discussions – one formal and one informal. For more information on how you will be assessed, see page 116.

This table shows you the 'standards', or assessment objectives, that your speaking, listening and communication will be assessed against.

Level 1 Skill standard for speaking, listening and communication: *Take full part in formal and informal discussions and exchanges that include unfamiliar subjects*
Make relevant and extended contributions to discussion, allowing for and responding to others' input
Make different kinds of contributions to discussions
Present information/points of view clearly and in appropriate language

Taking part in an informal discussion

This lesson will help you to:
- prepare for a discussion
- make clear, relevant contributions
- listen to others

You are going to discuss this topic:

> Your local council wants to teach children aged 8 to 11 about road safety. You have been asked to discuss what road safety advice you think should be given to them.

Watch out!

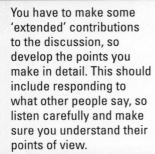

You have to make some 'extended' contributions to the discussion, so develop the points you make in detail. This should include responding to what other people say, so listen carefully and make sure you understand their points of view.

Key skills for discussions

Before you start, remind yourself of some key skills for discussions:

- Think about what your audience needs to know and prepare some points.
- Organise what you say. Begin with a main point then give more detail.
- Listen carefully and actively when others are speaking.
- Speak clearly and politely. Use correct grammar and avoid slang words.
- Explain unusual words or difficult ideas. Explain technical terms (jargon).
- Check that your audience understands you. Ask 'Is that clear?' or 'Are there any questions?'

Step 1 Prepare and organise your points

1   Come up with six points that children should learn about road safety, such as looking both ways before crossing the road. Choose two points that you will use in the discussion.

2   **a** Work out how you can explain your two points clearly. Make sure you can add details, perhaps by giving examples. Make notes that you can use while you are speaking, such as those on the right:

    b Practise explaining each of your points out loud. Make your main point first, then add the details.

Notes

cycle helmet

hi-vis armbands

Main point – wear safety clothing

bright clothes in the dark

3   Work in a group.

    a Take turns explaining the first of your road safety points.

    b Listen to other people's points. Give them feedback. You could fill in a table like the one below.

Skills used – the speaker...	✓ if used	Examples
Gave a clear explanation of the point		
Organised information clearly and gave details		
Checked listeners' understanding		
Used words that people understood		
Explained unusual words/ideas		
Spoke at the right pace (not too fast/slow)		
Spoke at the right volume (not too loud/soft)		

    c Study the feedback you are given for your own points. What skills do you need to improve on?

Step 2 Active listening

Active listening means you should:

▶ Pay close attention to what someone is saying.

▶ Respond to the speaker in your body language.

▶ Make short comments to show that you are listening.

▶ Ask questions or summarise to check your understanding.

Work in your group. Take turns explaining your second idea to one person in your group. The other people should check the skills of the listener by filling in a table like the one below.

Skills used – the listener...	✓ if used	Examples
Paid close attention		
Showed interest in their facial expressions and body language		
Made short comments		
Asked questions or summarised		

Step 3 Make effective contributions

Activity 3

1 Read the speech bubbles below.

2 Discuss them in your group.
 a What is done well?
 b What needs more practice?
 Give reasons for your views, for example 'This speaker made a clear point, but the next person did not respond politely.'

Group A

> I think children need to find a safe place to cross the road.

> Yes, I agree. They should be told to use a zebra crossing.

> Me auntie got knocked over at a zebra. She were well hurt, like.

Group B

> What else should children learn? What do you think Ellie?

> They shouldn't stand in between parked cars to cross because drivers won't see them.

> Don't be stupid. No one's going to walk half a mile to find an empty space.

Group C

> Children need to keep listening and looking while they are crossing just in case a car appears.

> I can see your point, but how can you make them do that?

> We could ask them questions – 'A car appears when you are halfway across. What should you do?' What do you think?

Top tip

Asking questions is a good way to keep the discussion flowing. Show that it is important to you to understand what others think, as well as to be understood by them.

Step 4 Have your discussion

Remind yourself of the discussion topic on page 46.

During the discussion, make sure you:

▶ Play a full part, but don't do all the talking.

▶ Actively listen to others.

▶ Make relevant points that fit in with the task and what others are saying.

▶ Say when you agree with or support others, for example 'I agree that…' or 'I can see what you mean…'.

▶ Say when you disagree with others and put your own viewpoint, for example 'But don't you think…' or 'I can see your point, but…'.

▶ Speak politely and clearly. This is an informal discussion, but you should still try to speak correctly and avoid too much slang.

▶ Help others by asking questions, for example 'Hamid, what do you think?'.

▶ Remember the feedback you got earlier and use it to improve your skills.

> ### Activity 4
>
> Have the full discussion in your group. Remember to use the points you have prepared.

Step 5 Assess your skills

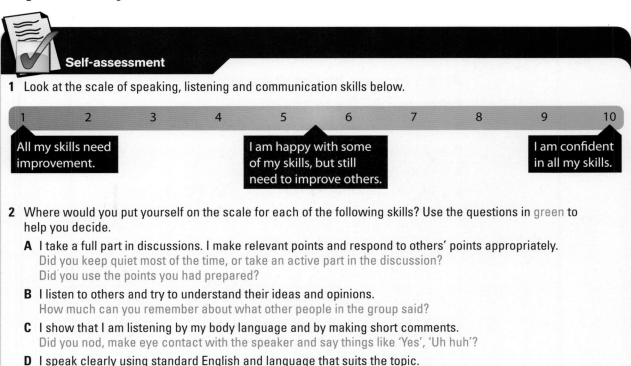

Self-assessment

1 Look at the scale of speaking, listening and communication skills below.

1	2	3	4	5	6	7	8	9	10

All my skills need improvement.

I am happy with some of my skills, but still need to improve others.

I am confident in all my skills.

2 Where would you put yourself on the scale for each of the following skills? Use the questions in green to help you decide.

A I take a full part in discussions. I make relevant points and respond to others' points appropriately.
Did you keep quiet most of the time, or take an active part in the discussion?
Did you use the points you had prepared?

B I listen to others and try to understand their ideas and opinions.
How much can you remember about what other people in the group said?

C I show that I am listening by my body language and by making short comments.
Did you nod, make eye contact with the speaker and say things like 'Yes', 'Uh huh'?

D I speak clearly using standard English and language that suits the topic.
Did you use slang? How did you check that other people in the group understood you?

3 a Work in your group using the skills you have learned. Discuss each person's scores.
  b Help each person to set a goal for improvement in their discussion skills.

2 Taking part in a formal discussion

This lesson will help you to:
▶ prepare for a discussion
▶ take part in a formal discussion, adopting different roles

Top tip

Research the topic before the discussion so you can be confident of the facts and be sure of your own ideas on the subject.

You are going to discuss this topic:

> Your group has to choose one charity that your school or college should fundraise for this year. Choose from the charities described opposite, and any others that you know about.

Step 1 Prepare for the discussion

Before your discussion, you should:

▶ Take time to think about what you will say.

▶ Read relevant information. Plan what points you will make.

▶ Decide who will chair the discussion.

▶ Prepare an agenda by deciding in which order different parts of the discussion will happen. For example, in which order you will look at the different charities?

Activity 1

1 Use the information about Charities A, B and C opposite for this activity.

2 **a** On your own, decide which charity you want to support.
   b Work out your reasons and make brief notes.

3 Work with a partner who has chosen the same charity as you. Decide on four points you could make at the meeting to support your choice .

4 What points could be made to support the other charities? Work out how you could oppose those points if they are made in the discussion.

Charity A

Music in Hospitals

Creating joy through live music

Music in Hospitals' mission is to improve the quality of life of children and adults living with illness and disability through the joy and therapeutic benefits of live music.

Live music can improve the quality of life for patients, residents, and carers by enhancing the environment within which they live and work.

5 Music in Hospitals arranges in the region of 5,000 concerts each year in hospital wards, day rooms, lounges, halls and by the bedsides of patients who are too ill to be moved.

The musicians do not provide miracle cures but magical moments of warmth and joy as they help to bring the person out of the patient. Find out more at www.musicinhospitals.org.uk

Charity B

NATIONAL ECZEMA SOCIETY

The **National Eczema Society** offers help and information to everyone affected by eczema.

It has an eczema helpline and a website, and produces a magazine giving advice and information to sufferers.

5 It runs support groups for children and families living with eczema.

It gives information and advice to health professionals about eczema.

It provides information packs teachers can use in schools to help schools understand eczema and how it affects children.

Charity C

– Positive About Youth

http://www.positiveaboutyouth.org/

ukyouth Positive About Youth — CENTENARY YEAR

Home | About | Our supporters | Sign up and support "Positive about Youth" | Donate | Nigel Mansell Challenge | Hay Festival | Contact us | Events | Links

UK Youth is the leading national youth work charity supporting over 750,000 young people, helping them to raise their aspirations, realise their potential and have their achievements recognised via non-formal, accredited education programmes and activities.

5 This year UK Youth is 100 years old! We are using our centenary to promote a positive message about young people and to demonstrate that we value them. You can find out more and pledge your support at www.positiveaboutyouth.org

For further information go to www.ukyouth.org

Top tip

For top marks, you need to be able to contribute to the discussion in many different ways. This includes listening carefully and responding to other people's ideas as well as giving your own. Try to make sure everyone has a chance to put forward their views and help the group come to an agreement or decision about the topic under discussion.

Step 2 Make effective contributions

Contributing effectively doesn't just mean clearly stating your own views. You should also:

▶ Speak in standard English and avoid slang or dialect words.

▶ Give reasons for your views, such as '…because animals can't look after themselves'.

▶ Ask questions about others' views, such as 'Why do you think it's more important to…?'.

▶ Support or politely criticise others' points. For example, 'I understand what you are saying, but…'.

▶ Make sure everyone has a chance to speak. For example, 'Does anyone disagree?'

▶ Try to reach an agreement that suits most people, such as 'So, will everyone be happy if …?'.

Activity 2

1 Work with your partner and another pair who have chosen a different charity. Each of you should:
  a Make two points in support of your charity.
  b Make two points in response to other people's suggestions.

2 Give each other feedback. Read again the list under 'Make effective contributions' at the top of this page. What did you do well and what do you need to improve? Set yourself a goal.

Chairing a discussion

You may be asked to be the chairperson; this means running a discussion. As chairperson you should:

▶ Make sure contributions are relevant and move the discussion on if not.

▶ Make sure everyone contributes and invite people to speak. For example, 'Jamal, what do you think?'

▶ Sum up the discussion at the end. For example, 'So, we have decided…'.

▶ Make sure the discussion sticks to the time allowed. For example, 'We need to move on now…'.

▶ Deal with any disrespectful behaviour. For example, 'Please can we all listen quietly to…'.

Activity 3

1 Role-play a short discussion and take turns to be the chairperson. Practise each of the skills listed above, such as moving the discussion on if a point is not relevant.

2 In your group, decide who is to chair your discussion.

Step 3 Write an agenda

An agenda is a document used for formal discussions. It states:

▶ the aim of the discussion   ▶ who will attend   ▶ what needs to be covered.

Activity 4

In your group, write an agenda for your discussion. You can make it look like the example below.

AGENDA

Aim: To decide which charity Lanyon College should fundraise for in 2012

Group members: Toby Farrell, Efua Bello, Gea Liu, Ben Smith

Item number	Item	Introduced by
1	Introduction to the meeting	Chairperson – Efua
2	Music in Hospitals	Toby

Step 4 Have your discussion

Remind yourself of the discussion topic on page 50.

Activity 5

Have the discussion in your group. After ten minutes the chairperson should end the discussion and sum up any decisions.

Step 5 Assess your skills

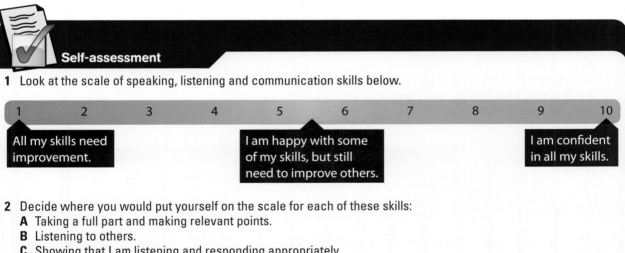

Self-assessment

1 Look at the scale of speaking, listening and communication skills below.

| 1 | 2 | 3 | 4 | 5 | 6 | 7 | 8 | 9 | 10 |

All my skills need improvement.

I am happy with some of my skills, but still need to improve others.

I am confident in all my skills.

2 Decide where you would put yourself on the scale for each of these skills:
   A Taking a full part and making relevant points.
   B Listening to others.
   C Showing that I am listening and responding appropriately.
   D Speaking clearly, using standard English.
3 If you were chairperson, decide where you would put yourself on the scale for:
   A Keeping everyone to the subject.
   B Making sure everyone contributed appropriately.
   C Reaching group decisions on time.
4 As a group, set an improvement target for each person.

Speaking, listening and communication practice tasks

▶ Look at the examples of the kinds of tasks you may be given in your speaking, listening and communication assessments.

▶ Use the examiner's tips and the self-assessment checklist on pages 56–57 to develop your skills in taking part in formal and informal discussions.

Informal discussion

In pairs or small groups, discuss the best and worst things about living in your area.

I've lived here all my life so I've got lots of friends and family near me.

I moved here a few years ago and I still miss friends from my old home.

I wish there was more to do. It's quite a long journey to the town centre for the shops and cinema.

There's lots of crime where I live. I don't feel safe going out at night.

Top tip

Give your own views clearly, using appropriate language and explain your comments in detail, giving examples if necessary. Remember to listen to what other people are saying. Try to understand their point of view, for example by asking questions.

Don't let the discussion get stuck by going over and over the same point. Think about what you need to achieve and keep the discussion moving forward.

Formal discussion

Your school or college has decided to hold a 'Green Day' with a variety of activities aimed at making the school greener. Each class has been asked to take part in at least one activity involving either the whole class or smaller groups.

In a group of up to five, discuss possible activities and decide on **two** you would recommend to the rest of your class.

Use the prompts below to help you.

> We could make every lesson have a 'green' theme and focus on learning about ways of helping the environment.

> If everyone walked or cycled to school, or at least organised a car share, it would cut down on greenhouse gases.

> What about working out how much energy we use each week as a class? It might encourage people to cut down if they knew how much they were using.

> Maybe we could have a competition for the best example of something made from recycled objects, such as a lampshade made from a clothes hanger and scraps of cloth, or a sculpture made out of tin cans and plastic bags.

Top tip

- Make sure you are clear about you audience and purpose, and what kind of languge you should use.
- Prepare the points you want to make. Write a list of your own ideas and do some research on the internet if you need to. Be ready to back up your ideas with evidence, if possible.

In a successful discussion, everyone must play a part. At different times you could:
- **Start** the discussion:
  - organise the group
  - help to plan the task.
- **Develop** the discussion:
  - ask questions
  - ask for a point to be explained
  - challenge other people's ideas
  - suggest alternatives of your own.
- **Lead** the discussion:
  - make sure everybody in the group has a chance to speak
  - summarise the range of different views and suggestions
  - help to settle disagreements.

Self-assessment

1 When you have completed the discussion tasks, reflect on your own performance. Use the tips from the examiner to help you.

2 On your own or with a partner, use the checklist on these pages to mark your performance. To achieve a Level 1 for Speaking, listening and communication, you need to be able to say 'Yes' to most or all of the points on the checklist.

3 Help each other to set goals for improvement:

• Where you ticked 'sometimes', think about the times that you did not demonstrate the skill. What can you do to improve?

  For example, if sometimes you do not listen carefully to what other people are saying, think about what might be preventing you from doing this. Practise your listening skills by repeating the main points of what others have said to check you have understood them correctly.

• Where you ticked 'no', set yourself the goal of practising the skill. Review the relevant parts of pages 44 to 55. Try practising the skill informally.

  For example, if you used too much slang ask a partner to listen to you and put their hand up every time you do so. Then think of a better word you could use. Keep practising until you are confident of the skill.

Self-assessment checklist

	Yes	Sometimes	No
Do I show I have been listening carefully by linking my own comments and questions clearly to what others have said?			
Do I use the correct scientific or technical terms where necessary and avoid using slang terms which might not be understood by everyone?			
Can I explain my ideas clearly so my audience understands and is persuaded to share my views?			
Can I match my words, volume and tone of voice to suit the age, level of confidence, ability and knowledge of my audience?			
In discussions, do I pay attention to others' views and what the group is trying to achieve?			
Can I make and explain relevant points clearly?			
Do I encourage others to put their views forward and support their ideas by comments, questions or non-verbal means?			
Can I help to keep discussions moving forward towards a decision and to resolve disagreements within the group?			
Can I confidently participate in discussions, including those with people I am unfamiliar with? For example: • presenting my own ideas clearly • listening attentively • encouraging and supporting others • negotiating • leading • record-keeping			

Introduction to writing

The texts and activities in this section of the book will help you to develop your skills in writing. You will:

- think about audience, purpose, form and style
- learn how to plan and organise your writing
- learn how to use main points and details to make your writing effective
- use paragraphs and sentences to present your writing clearly and logically.

At the end of the section you will find two writing tasks. These will help you to practise and assess your writing skills in the kinds of questions you will meet in the test. There are also sample answers at Pass and Fail, with comments from the examiner. For a full practice test, see pages 126 to 127.

ResultsPlus
Self-assessment

For each unit of work, you will be given learning objectives. Read these carefully before you start, and work out how confident you feel about your skills in each area. At the end of each unit, think about how your skills have improved. What still needs further practice?

Your assessment

You will be assessed in one 45-minute test. You will be asked to complete two writing tasks. For more information on how you will be assessed, see page 114.

This table shows you the 'standards', or assessment objectives, that your writing will be assessed against.

Level 1 Skill standard for writing: *Write a range of texts to communicate information, ideas and opinions, using formats and styles suitable for their purpose and audience.*
Write clearly and coherently, including an appropriate level of detail
Present information in a logical sequence
Use language, format and structure suitable for purpose and audience
Use correct grammar, including correct and consistent use of tense
Ensure written work includes generally accurate punctuation and spelling and that meaning is clear

Planning your writing: a summary of text types

Use the grid below to help you as you work through the tasks in this writing section and in your assessments. It will help you to plan an effective piece of writing.

For any writing task you are given:

▶ First identify the words in the task that show the purpose by using column 1. For example, if the question uses the word 'telling', your purpose may be to instruct.
▶ Then check what format to write in (some examples are given in column three).
▶ Practise using the features given in column four to plan and shape your text.

Purpose Your purpose could be to:	Key words The task might use words such as:	Format You might be asked to write a:
instruct/advise/ request	telling, asking, booking, inviting, giving advice, giving suggestions, giving directions	notice leaflet letter e-mail
inform/explain	informing, explaining, describing, stating	leaflet letter e-mail article
		briefing note
argue	arguing, complaining, requesting, giving your views/opinions	letter article leaflet speech
discuss	discussing, commenting	article speech podcast

Features
Remember to include these features:

Title: state what you are writing about
Main section: write clearly your purpose and relevant information
Without forgetting: appropriate layout features for letters

Title: state what you are writing about
Main section: give the information in a logical order. You can use subheadings and bulleted or numbered lists

Title: give a factual heading
Introduction: state the topic
Background: give a brief explanation, information, history
Considerations: explain the facts/issues

Introduction: state the topic
Main section: give the facts and give your views
Conclusion: sum up your viewpoint and ask for actions

Introduction: state the topic of the discussion
Main section: give information for and against
Conclusion: sum up the issues and suggest actions

Writing for your audience

ResultsPlus
Top tip

In the exam, read the task carefully and underline the words in the question that tell you about the audience. As you write keep checking that your writing is suitable.

The audience is the person or people who will read your text. Always read the writing task carefully and ask yourself:

▶ Who am I writing for (the audience)?

▶ What does this audience need to know?

▶ How can I make sure my format, content and language suit this audience?

Activity 1

1 Who is the audience for the task below?

> Write a letter to your local council, suggesting ways of improving your area for young adults.

2 Read the following notes that one student has made for the task.

A Audience: the local council. Adult officials who need clear information to make decisions.
B They need to know what my ideas are and how they would improve the area:

C Language to suit this audience: they're officials and I want them to take my ideas seriously. Need formal standard English in letter format. Not slang.

3 What else should this student do to suit the audience for this task? Make a list of the points you would add to make sure you write a really good letter.

Activity 2

1 Read Tasks A, B and C below. For each of the tasks, decide who the audience is.

> **Task A** Should people be allowed to talk on their mobile phone while driving? Join in the discussion on a website for drivers by posting a message.
>
> **Task B** Should the school-leaving age be lowered? Write a letter to your MP, arguing for or against the idea.
>
> **Task C** Your local council wants to begin emptying your rubbish bins only once a month. Write a letter to the council, arguing for rubbish bins to be emptied every week.

2 What does the audience of Task A need to know? Draw a spider diagram to show your ideas.

3 Which of the three tasks should you write in formal standard English?

Activity 3

1 a Read Task C again.

> **Task C** Your local council wants to begin emptying your rubbish bins only once a month. Write a letter to the council, arguing for rubbish bins to be emptied every week.

2 What does the audience of the task need to know?

3 What language would suit this audience?

4 Compare your ideas with what the students have written below. Which student do you think has best suited their writing to the audience? Give reasons.

> Rubbish left in bins for a long time will rot. Rats, flies and other animals will try to eat the rubbish. Rats and flies spread diseases. It is not healthy to leave rubbish lying around for such long periods.

> There'll be rats everywhere and the whole place will stink. It'll be like some slum you see on Comic Relief. No way should we end up living like this.

5 Write your own paragraph for Task C. Make sure its form, content and language suit the audience.

Writing to suit a purpose

Results Plus
Watch out!

If you are not clear about why you are writing, what you write may not be fit for purpose and you will lose marks. Look for information in the task that tells you what your writing needs to achieve. Ask yourself, 'What do I want my readers to think, feel or do when they read this?'

Your purpose is your reason for writing, for example to inform or explain. Work out what you need to put in your text so that it achieves its purpose. Ask yourself these questions:

What do I need to do for this audience? (For example, do they need the facts about something?)

What do I want the audience to do? (For example, agree with my point of view.)

What do I have to include in my writing to achieve my purpose? (For example, evidence to support my point of view.)

Activity 1

1 Read Tasks A, B and C below.

Task A Write a leaflet telling tourists about two interesting places to visit in your area.

Task B Write a web page advising young adults about three different ways to save money.

Task C Write a letter persuading an employer to pay 16- and 20-year-old employees the same rate. (At the moment 16-year-olds are paid £1 an hour less.)

2 Decide what the purpose of each of the above tasks is.

Activity 2

1 Read Task A again.

> **Task A** Write a leaflet telling tourists about two interesting places to visit in your area.

2 What do you need to do for the audience of this task?

3 What do you want the audience to do?

4 What do you have to include to achieve your purpose? You could look at the table on pages 58 to 59 to give you some ideas.

Activity 3

1 Read Task B again.

> **Task B** Write a web page advising young adults about three different ways to save money.

2 What do you need to do for the audience of this task?

3 Look at the following student's notes for the task. Which three points do you think they should include so that the audience has what it needs?

B Check out the best prices for anything you need to buy using a web search tool such as www.pricechecker.com.

A Sell your junk at a car boot sale or through eBay.

C Consider buying supermarkets' own brands – they are usually cheaper.

Ways to save money

F It's important to treat yourself so you feel good. Don't save all the time.

D Buy in bulk – usually this is cheaper.

E Buy a lot of the goods you normally use when they have special offers on, such as buy one get one free.

ResultsPlus
Top tip

If possible, give supporting evidence for your facts, for example 'according to a recent BBC survey…'.

Using facts and opinions

A **fact** is a piece of information that can be proved to be true; for example, 16-year-old employees are paid less than 20-year-old employees.

An **opinion** is someone's point of view; for example, 16-year-olds should earn as much as 20-year-olds.

You need to know the purpose of your text in order to be able to decide whether to include facts or opinions. For example, an information text should include facts. Persuasive writing may include opinions supported by facts.

Activity 1

1 Decide whether the following statements are facts or opinions.
   A No one should buy clothes that have been made in sweatshops.
   B Clothes made in sweatshops are cheap to produce.
   C Workers in sweatshops are not allowed to belong to unions.
   D It's terrible that children have to work so their families have food.

2 Add a fact to the following opinion to make it more persuasive:
   Child workers who miss school cannot escape from poverty because…

3 a Read the following student's draft paragraph of an article on child workers. Its purpose is to persuade the reader that child labour is wrong.

No one should be forced to work in a sweatshop making clothes. It gives people in the West cheap clothes, but it keeps people in countries such as India, Africa and China poor. Women and children suffer most. The factory owners should be made to pay them a fair wage and to make sure the children get an education.

   b Identify an opinion. How could this student improve their writing by backing up this opinion with a fact?

Activity 2

1 Read Task C again.

> **Task C** Write a letter persuading an employer to pay
> 16- and 20-year-old employees the same rate. (At the
> moment 16-year-olds are paid £1 an hour less.)

2 a Make a plan for this task, answering the following questions:
- What is my purpose for writing?
- What do I need to do for this audience?
- What do I want the audience to do?

b Now decide on two points you could include so that your text will achieve its purpose.

c Finally, decide how to include facts to back up your points.

3 a Swap plans with a partner. Do you think their plan would achieve its purpose? Give reasons.

b Suggest at least one way of improving your partner's plan to make it more likely to achieve its purpose.

Activity 3

1 Read Task D below.

> **Task D** Write an article for a school magazine, arguing that
> the legal age for driving should be raised to 21.

2 a Make a short plan listing your purpose, what the audience needs and what you want the audience to do.

b Decide on two points you want to make.

c How could you use some of the facts below to back up your points?
- Teenage drivers make up only 7 per cent of all drivers, but are involved in 14 per cent of all fatal car crashes every year.
- Teenagers are less likely to be wearing a safety belt than older drivers.
- Teenagers are more likely to drive while under the influence of drugs or alcohol.
- Teenage drivers are more likely to become distracted while driving.

3 Swap plans with a partner and discuss what works well and what could be improved.

Results Plus
Top tip

The features of different forms of writing help the reader to find the information they are looking for. Using these features correctly will make your writing more effective and get you more marks.

Writers use different forms for different purposes. Some examples of forms are:

▶ a letter
▶ an article
▶ an email
▶ a leaflet.

Always read a writing task carefully. It will tell you in which form your text should be written.

Activity 1

1 Read Tasks A and B below.

2 What form of writing would you use if you were asked to respond to each task?

Task A You are going on holiday and have noticed that some of the details on your travel documents are incorrect. Write to the travel company asking them to supply corrected documents.

Task B New students need to know how to use the facilities at your school or college. Write some advice on how to use the library.

Different texts have different features, such as headings or lists. You should use the features that are suitable for the form of writing you are asked to produce. Work through pages 69 to 73 to learn more about some different forms of writing.

Activity 2

Look at Text A below. It is an example of a formal letter. Some key features of formal letters have been explained for you.

1 Use Text A below for this activity.

2 Check your understanding of how to lay out letters by answering the following questions.
  a Where do you place your own address?
  b What words do you use to sign off?
  c Where do you place the date?
  d Where do you place the address of the person you are writing to?

3 Now look at the content of the two paragraphs in the letter. Complete these sentences:
  a The opening paragraph states what the letter…
  b The closing paragraph says what the writer…

Text A

29 Warren Grove
Egton
Essex
CM71 1ER

> The sender's address and the date go here.

21st August 2010

Mr Paul Keats
Waste Collection Manager
Egton Borough Council
High Street
Egton
EA3 IS4

> The name and address of the person receiving the letter go here.

Dear Mr Keats

> Formal letters begin 'Dear…'

I wish to complain. My rubbish bins have not been emptied for over a month now. I have had to drive sacks of rubbish to the dump so that we do not get rats.

I pay my council tax and I expect to get the services I pay for. Please make sure my bins will be emptied from now on.

Yours sincerely

> Sign off like this. If you don't know the name of the person you're writing to, sign off 'Yours faithfully'.

Bill Bodrun

ResultsPlus
Watch out!

Published articles are often set out in columns but don't try to do this in the exam. Handwriting makes narrow columns difficult to write and difficult to read. Don't waste time drawing images either – these will not be considered as part of your writing.

Activity 4

1 Look at Text B below. It is an example of a magazine article. Some features of articles have been pointed out for you.

2 Check your understanding of how to write articles by answering the following questions.
   a What does the heading of the article tell you?
   b How does the first sentence draw the reader in?
   c Each paragraph gives a new main point. What is the main point of paragraph 2?
   d What is the main point of paragraph 4? How does the writer back up this point?

The heading.

Text B

A gadget-free week

The first paragraph introduces the topic in an interesting way.

Could you live without your favourite gadgets for a fortnight? What would you do with all the time you would save by not playing
5 with your PlayStation or going on Facebook? This was the challenge faced by a class of students at Ecclestone College.

Quotations are used as evidence for the points made.

The first few days were the
10 hardest. 'I felt lost without my mobile phone,' said Aneeka. The teenagers' parents found it hard too: 'Sam kept moaning he had nothing to do. But then he decided to go out and play some sport instead of sitting in front of the
15 screen all day,' said one parent.

Each paragraph makes a new point.

Many of the students complained that they were bored at the beginning of the fortnight. As Theo said, 'I think it shows we've got quite lazy. When you have to change, everyone moans. But by the end of the first week I'd actually talked to my brother about
20 something other than Grand Theft Auto.'

By the end of the fortnight everyone could see some benefits. Keren seems to sum it up for a lot of people. 'I felt a lot less stressed – I don't know why. I even got more homework done.'

The final paragraph sums up.

At the end of the fortnight people were pleased to see their
25 gadgets again, but hopefully they will choose to turn them off or leave them at home sometimes and enjoy a bit of calm.

Activity 5

1 Look at Text C below. It is an example of an email. Some features of emails have been pointed out for you.

2 Check your understanding of how to write emails by answering the following questions.
  a How do you begin a formal email?
  b What do you need to put in the first paragraph?
  c How do you make it clear what you want the reader to do?

Text C

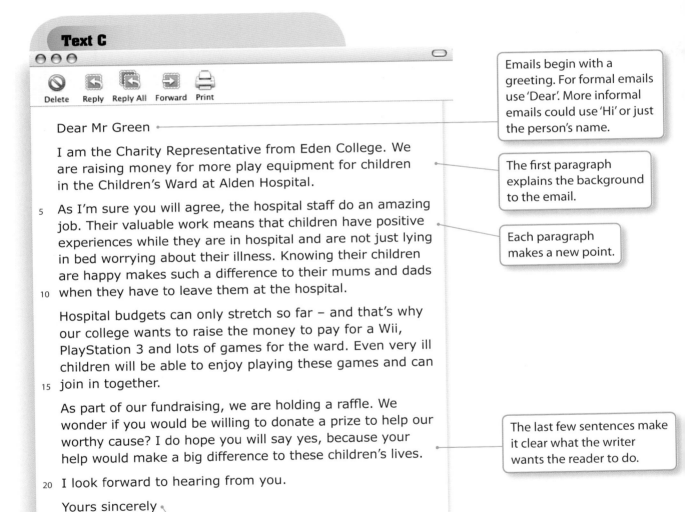

Dear Mr Green

I am the Charity Representative from Eden College. We are raising money for more play equipment for children in the Children's Ward at Alden Hospital.

5 As I'm sure you will agree, the hospital staff do an amazing job. Their valuable work means that children have positive experiences while they are in hospital and are not just lying in bed worrying about their illness. Knowing their children are happy makes such a difference to their mums and dads
10 when they have to leave them at the hospital.

Hospital budgets can only stretch so far – and that's why our college wants to raise the money to pay for a Wii, PlayStation 3 and lots of games for the ward. Even very ill children will be able to enjoy playing these games and can
15 join in together.

As part of our fundraising, we are holding a raffle. We wonder if you would be willing to donate a prize to help our worthy cause? I do hope you will say yes, because your help would make a big difference to these children's lives.

20 I look forward to hearing from you.

Yours sincerely

Adam Oakley

Emails begin with a greeting. For formal emails use 'Dear'. More informal emails could use 'Hi' or just the person's name.

The first paragraph explains the background to the email.

Each paragraph makes a new point.

The last few sentences make it clear what the writer wants the reader to do.

When the email is quite formal, the ending should be like this. More informal emails could end with just your name, or 'Love' or 'Best wishes'.

1 Look at Text D below. It is an example of a leaflet giving advice. Some features of leaflets have been pointed out for you.

2 Check your understanding of how to write leaflets by answering the following questions.

   a Why does a leaflet need a title?

   b What should the first paragraph do?

   c This leaflet uses a bulleted list for information. How else might you lay out information so that it is easy for the reader to follow?

Text D

The title tells the reader what the leaflet is about.

Using a taxi safely

There is an introduction to the topic in the first paragraph.

Make sure your evening out ends happily. Plan how to get home before you go. If you are going to use a taxi, remember these tips.

Lists of key points can help the reader to understand the information.

- Always use a registered taxi or minicab.
5 - Carry the telephone number of a registered taxi service you know you can trust.
- Try to book your taxi in advance.
- Ask for the driver's name and details of what car he or she will be driving.
10 - If possible, share the taxi with a friend.
- Check the estimated fare with the driver before you set off.
- Always sit in the back of the taxi.

Use what you have learnt about different writing forms to make revision cards.

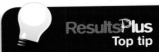

Activity 7

ResultsPlus
Top tip

The form your writing should take is sometimes suggested by the layout of the answer pages on your exam paper. For example, they may be laid out to look like a letter heading, email or questionnaire.

1 Use Texts A, B, C and D for this activity.

2 a Look again at Text A on page 69 and the notes around it. Write 'Formal letter' at the top of a blank sheet of card or paper.

b Now list what to include when you are writing a formal letter. Use the example below to get you started.

> *Formal letter*
>
> *1 Has two addresses:*
> - *Mine goes at the top right with the date under it.*
> - *The reader's address goes below that on the left.*

c You could include a sketch showing the main features. Use the example below to get you started.

3 Now make revision cards for each of Texts B, C and D on pages 70, 71 and 72.

4 a Swap cards with a partner. Check that they have included all the right features. Make corrections if you need to.

b Test each other to see if you can remember the features of the different forms.

4 Understanding style

Read a writing task carefully to work out how formal your writing needs to be. Look for the key words that tell you about the audience, purpose and form of the task.

Results**Plus**
Watch out!

Make sure you match your tone to the task. If you are writing for a serious purpose or you do not know the audience you are writing for very well, you need to use a formal tone in your writing. Avoid using text speak (e.g. LOL), slang (e.g. OK) or dialect words (e.g. bairn). Always use correct grammar and punctuation.

You should use a **formal** style if:
1 Your audience is an organisation, for example a business, local council, school or charity.
2 Your purpose is official or legal, for example to apply for a job or make a complaint.
3 You are asked to write in a formal form, for example a formal letter or a briefing note.

You should use a more **informal** style if:
1 You know your audience personally, for example a family member, teacher or fellow students.
2 Your purpose is to seem friendly and approachable, for example to persuade a friend to help you in a charity event.
3 You are asked to write in an informal form, for example an email.

Activity 1

1 Read Tasks A, B, C and D below. For each task, find the key words that tell you about form, purpose and audience. The first one has been done for you.

> Form – leaflet.

> Audience – students.

> Purpose – explaining how to present themselves.

Task A Write a leaflet for students explaining how they should present themselves well during work experience.

Task B Write a report for the government on what life skills you think teenagers should be taught before they are 16.

Task C Write an article for a parenting magazine discussing raising the school-leaving age to 18.

Task D Write an email to one of your teachers suggesting a suitable trip for students.

2 For each of Tasks A to D, decide whether you should use a formal or an informal style.

Formal standard English
- ▶ Use correct grammar.
- ▶ Do not use any dialect or slang.
- ▶ Use sophisticated or technical words.
- ▶ Keep your writing impersonal.

For example:

> Dear Sir,
>
> I understand that Printworks offers students work experience in printing. I would very much like to work in this area when I leave school. For this reason I am already studying relevant GCSEs.

Less formal standard English
- ▶ Use correct grammar.
- ▶ Do not use dialect or slang.
- ▶ Include some informal words such as *don't* or *can't*.
- ▶ Use common, everyday words.
- ▶ Your writing can be more personal and direct.

For example:

> Hi
> I've written to the manager at Printworks to ask if I can do my work experience with them. Hopefully I'll find out what it's really like – and they might have a job going for me later on. What do you think?

Activity 2

1 Read Task A again.

> **Task A** Write a leaflet for students explaining how they should present themselves well during work experience.

2 a Read these students' first drafts of some ideas for this task.

> Students have to decide what kind of impression they want to create in the workplace. To be treated as a professional, they should dress like one.

> Some people don't know which colours or shapes really suit them.

> If you try to dress like a celebrity, you may stand out at work for the wrong reasons. This is especially true if there is a company dress code everyone has to follow.

> It's fun to try on a totally different look in a shop changing room. Work experience students should go for it!

b Which of the drafts above are written in formal standard English?
c Give reasons for your answers. Use the information in the boxes at the top of this page to help you.

3 Rewrite the informal drafts so that they are in formal standard English.

Review what you have learnt about formal and informal style, then work through the activities on this page.

Activity 3

1 Read Task B again.

> **Task B** Write a report for the government on what life skills you think teenagers should be taught before they are 16.

2 a Now read Ryan's first draft for this task.

> I think everyone should learn how to cook before they leave school. I don't mean just being able to stick a pizza and chips in the oven. Even if that's how you choose to eat, you should know that you can do something different if you want to. It's better for you to cook things like pasta or a roast chicken dinner than living on takeaways and microwave dinners, isn't it?

b What changes should Ryan make so that his style better suits his task?
c Write a second draft of his text in a more appropriate style.

3 a Write your own opening paragraph for this task, taking care to suit your style to the audience, purpose and form.
b Swap finished paragraphs with a partner. Discuss whether you have each written in an appropriate style. Suggest any improvements you could make.

Using apostrophes

When you are writing less formal English you may use words like *don't, can't, wouldn't*. These are contractions of two more formal words, with an apostrophe to show where letters have been left out.

do not ➡ don't
can not ➡ can't
would not ➡ wouldn't

Activity 4

1 Read Task D again.

> **Task D** Write an email to one of your teachers suggesting a suitable trip for students.

2 Sunil has written the first draft of an email in response to Task D. Make his text less formal by contracting the highlighted words using an apostrophe.

You could take your PE GCSE students to the Snow Dome in Tamworth. Students would not need any special clothing or equipment, just warm clothes and gloves. It is really good value and you do not have to know how to ski or snowboard before you go.

At Tamworth, they have lots of instructors who can teach a whole group. Any students who do not want a lesson can still enjoy adrenalin tubing, ice skating and tobogganing. You will need to book ahead, and you must not forget that they have a Santa's Winter Wonderland from mid-November to early January, so the ice track and mini-rink are not available during that time.

You also need to use an apostrophe to show ownership. For example, 'the girl's jeans'.

If there is only one owner, just add an apostrophe and 's':
The snowboard belonging to one man ➡ The man's snowboard.

If there is more than one owner, look at the plural word being used:

If the plural ends in 's', just add an apostrophe:
The coats belonging to three girls ➡ The three girls' coats.

If the plural does not end in 's', add an apostrophe and 's':
The skates belonging to the women ➡ The women's skates.

Activity 5

1 Write a paragraph explaining what different people in your class could pack to take on a school trip. For example, for a weekend camping you could include Sam's tent, everyone's coats.

2 Read your paragraph and check that all the apostrophes are in the right places.

5 Planning and organising your writing

ResultsPlus
Top tip

Use the information you are given and the task itself to help you plan what you are going to write.

To write effectively, you must:

▶ Read the task carefully to make sure you are clear about your audience, your purpose, the form you should write in and what style is appropriate.

▶ Plan what to write carefully so that your text will be well organised and detailed.

Activity 1

1 Read Task A below. Some key words have been highlighted.

Task A

Information

Read the following messages on an internet discussion on whether parents should be allowed to smack their children.

> There's a big difference between a small tap on the hand after warning your child not to do something serious and beating them to death. Parents should be allowed to smack their children if it helps them learn to keep safe, e.g. not to run out on to the road. No one should ever beat their child.

> Hitting people is wrong. No one should ever hit anyone for any reason. If you hit a child you are teaching it that hitting people is all right.

Writing task

Write your own message to the internet discussion forum, in which you give your own detailed views on the subject.

---

2 Use the highlighted words in the task to help you to work out:
  a Your audience.
  b Your purpose.
  c What form you should write in, for example a letter or an email.
  d What style would be appropriate, for example formal or informal.

Gather and organise your ideas

Task A asks for your own detailed views on whether parents should smack children. Before you start writing you need to decide on:

▶ Your point of view.

▶ Some detailed points you can make to support your views.

Practise making a plan by working through Activity 2.

Activity 2

1 Write your point of view in the middle of a page, for example:

Smacking can help children
learn right and wrong.

2 Write these questions around your main point: Who? What? When? Where? Why? How? For example:

Who?

Where?

What? ——— Smacking can help children
learn right and wrong. ——— Why?

When? How?

These questions will help you to back up your point of view with detailed information.

3 Write an answer for each question, for example:

When?

Only when a child has done something wrong
that is dangerous, like run into the road.

4 Next to each of your answers, add a detail to back up your answer. For example:

When?

Only when a child has done something wrong
that is dangerous, like run into the road.
Because they'll learn that doing something
wrong will result in a punishment straight away,
so they'll stop doing it.

5 Decide which are your three strongest points. What is the best order to make them in? Number them 1 to 3.

6 Check your plan before you start writing. Is there anything you would like to add or change?

Activity 3

Now practise planning for a different task.

1 Read Task B below.

Task B

Information

The government wants to encourage children to eat more healthily and drink more water.

These are the main points it wants to make:

Healthy diet

1 Base your meals on starchy foods.
2 Eat lots of fruit and veg.
3 Eat more fish.
4 Cut down on saturated fat and sugar.
5 Try to eat less salt – no more than 6g a day.
6 Get active and try to be a healthy weight.
7 Drink plenty of water.
8 Don't skip breakfast.

Writing task

Write a letter to parents, suggesting ways they can help their children to eat more healthily. In your letter you should:

• explain why you are writing
• give information on how children can eat more healthily
• explain why it is important.

2 Work out the key words in the task that tell you:
  a Your audience.
  b Your purpose.
  c The form you should write in.

3 Decide whether you should use a formal or an informal style. Think about your purpose and audience to help you.

Gather and organise your ideas

For this task you are going to give examples of why parents should help children to eat healthily. Practise making a plan by working through Activity 4 below.

1 Use Task B opposite for this activity.

2 Write this statement in the middle of a page:

> Help your child to be
> healthy

3 Write these questions around your statement: Who? What? When? Where? Why? How?

4 Write an answer for each question. Use the information you were given in the task, for example:

What?

Eat breakfast.

5 Add at least one detail to back up each point, for example:

What?

Eat breakfast, so you won't be tempted by unhealthy snacks later in the morning.

6 Decide which points are your strongest. What is the best order to make them in? Number them in order of importance.

7 Check your plan. Have you included a detail for every point? Is there anything you would like to add or change?

6 Writing in paragraphs

When you plan your writing, you decide on the main points you want to make. You should start a new paragraph for each new main point. This will help your audience to follow your writing.

This lesson will help you to:
- plan your paragraphs
- write well-structured paragraphs
- link your paragraphs together

ResultsPlus
Top tip

Paragraphing helps to organise your writing. By grouping your ideas in separate paragraphs, you can develop each of your main points clearly.

Activity 1

1 Read Text A below.

2 Where should the writer have begun new paragraphs? Look carefully for where each new point starts to help you decide.

Text A

Sir,

There is far too much advertising these days. No wonder people are so unhappy when they keep getting shown amazing things that they cannot afford. Advertisers make people believe they are not
5 good enough if they have not got the latest product. Another lie is that 'everyone else has it so you should too'. This puts enormous pressure on people. Before Christmas children are bombarded with advertisements for every toy possible and then they pester their parents. It must be so hard for any parent to cope with all
10 that. Can it be good for us to become so greedy? We are never satisfied with what we have because we are always being tempted to want more more more! I think there should be more television and radio channels that do not have adverts, even if our licence fee has to go up. Then people could choose to be free from all
15 those campaigns and still enjoy their viewing and listening.

Yours faithfully

Tallula Streck

Structuring paragraphs

For a well-structured paragraph, you can include:

Point – the first sentence in the paragraph tells readers its main point.

Evidence – next give readers facts and/or anecdotes to prove that the point is sensible.

Explain – after giving evidence, explore its significance. Explain the main point in more depth or add other smaller points related to it.

Link – end the paragraph by showing how it links to the main topic or the point in the next paragraph.

To help you remember this, you can use the initial letters of the four points – PEEL.

Activity 2

1 Use Text B below for this activity. It is part of a text that is saying why advertising is not always a bad thing.

2 Read the text. The main point of the paragraph is highlighted for you.

3 Work out which part of the paragraph gives the evidence to back up the main point.

4 Which part adds more explanation of the evidence?

5 Which sentence links this point to the main point of the whole text?

Text B

Without advertising it would be difficult for people to choose what to buy. People learn about food products through TV advertising. They do not want to spend a lot of time working out what unfamiliar products to buy and adverts can help them to become familiar with what new products can offer. Anything that helps people to make informed choices cannot be all bad.

Activity 3

1 Use Text B above for this activity.

2 Read the following point, evidence and explanation for a new paragraph:

Point: Advertising is good for employment.
Evidence: Many people have jobs creating advertising campaigns.
Explanation: Jobs in advertising include scriptwriting, acting, filming and catering.

3 Use them to write your own paragraph.

4 The overall point of Text B is that advertising is not all bad. Add a sentence at the end of your paragraph to link it to this overall point.

Linking your ideas

You need to know how to:

▶ Link your ideas within your paragraphs.

▶ Link each paragraph to the next one.

To do this, use connectives (linking words). Here are some common connectives:

> To show the **order** that things happen in, use connectives such as:
>
> **first   next   then   later   finally**

> To add something to **support** a point you have already made, use connectives such as:
>
> **in addition   also   too**

> To **explain** your point or give reasons for it, use connectives such as:
>
> **because   so   for example**

> To add something to **go against** a point you have already made, use connectives such as:
>
> **however   but   on the other hand**

> To list your points by their **importance**, use connectives such as:
>
> **first   second   finally**

Work through Activities 4 and 5 to practise using these different kinds of connectives.

Activity 4

1 Imagine you are writing an advice web page for students about going to a festival.

2 Use 'order' connectives to put these four sentences in the right order for your opening paragraph:
   • Book your tickets.
   • Have fun when you get there.
   • Decide which festival you want to attend.
   • Make sure you can get there on time.
   For example, you could start:

   First, decide which festival you want to attend.

3 Add something to one of your sentences, using one of the 'support' connectives. For example:

   First, decide which festival you want to attend. Check which bands are playing too.

4 Add a reason, using one of the 'explain' connectives. For example:

   First, decide which festival you want to attend. Check which bands are playing too, because you won't enjoy it otherwise.

5 Add a different argument, using one of the 'go against' connectives. For example:

   First, decide which festival you want to attend. Check which bands are playing too, because you won't enjoy it otherwise. However, don't forget that you might enjoy watching some new bands.

Activity 5

1 a Read this draft of a second paragraph for your web page. There are gaps where connectives are needed.

_____ if you are going to a festival it is a good idea to plan ahead _____ you have a safe, fun time. Go with a friend _____ it is more fun and _____ you will have someone watching out for you. When you arrive, work
5   out where the safety stations are _____ you know where to get help if you need it. You may be given a map, which will be useful. _____ it is not enough to just stick it in your pocket. Make sure you use it to find your way around safely.

b Decide on connectives to fill the gaps. Remember to think about what kinds of connectives are needed. Use the boxes on page 84 to help you.

2 a Read the following information on how to keep your belongings safe at a festival.
   • Your belongings will be safe if you follow some simple rules.
   • Travel light – leave anything valuable at home.
   • Do not carry credit cards or large amounts of cash.
   • Make sure you have enough cash for everything you need.
   • Keep your money, phone and keys on you rather than in a bag or purse.

b Use the information to write a third paragraph. Link your ideas using connectives.

c Add a point to support the final piece of information.

3 Write a final paragraph for your text about going to a festival. Remember to use connectives.

Results Plus
Top tip

Paragraphing helps to organise your writing. By grouping your ideas in separate paragraphs, you can develop each of your main points clearly.

7 Using main points and details

To write effective paragraphs, you need to include both main points and details. Begin with a main point that tells the reader what the rest of the paragraph is about, then add details giving evidence and explanations.

Activity 1

Look at Text A below. Some key features have been explained for you.

Text A

The main point.

Details supporting the main point.

> Your bike must have good brakes. Magura Hydraulic Rim Brakes are better than V brakes because there are no cables and they are very powerful.

Activity 2

1 Look at Text B below, including the pictures.

2 a Which are the main points and images?
b Which are details?

Text B

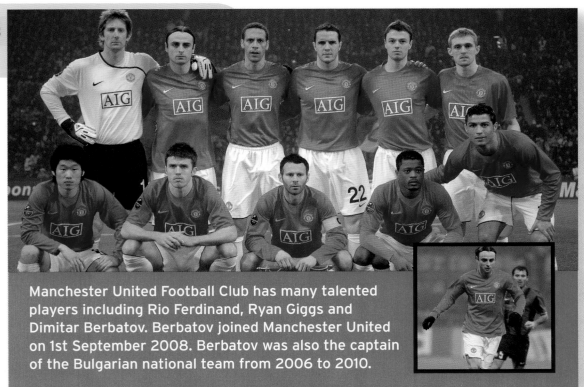

Manchester United Football Club has many talented players including Rio Ferdinand, Ryan Giggs and Dimitar Berbatov. Berbatov joined Manchester United on 1st September 2008. Berbatov was also the captain of the Bulgarian national team from 2006 to 2010.

1 Look at Text C below.

2 a What is the main point of paragraph 1?
b What detail supports the main point?

3 The main point of paragraph 3 is that Everton's U-9 side, with Rooney playing, beat Manchester's. What two details are given about Rooney's performance to support that point?

4 The main point of the final paragraph is that Rooney was to go on to be special. What detailed evidence is given of this?

Text C

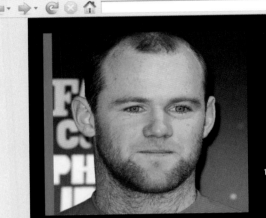

10 Wayne Rooney

1 **Wayne Rooney's face is familiar all over the world as a top striker for Manchester United and England.**

2 Rooney was born on 24th October 1985. He joined Everton's youth team at the age of 10, making his professional debut with the club in 2002. On 31st August 2004 he moved to Manchester United where he still plays the position of striker.

3 On his debut match with Manchester United he scored a hat-trick against Turkish club Fenerbahce, making himself instantly unforgettable. Rooney has since gone on to score a great number of goals for his club and his talent is recognised all over the world.

4 Rooney made his England debut in 2003 and has since been selected on a number of occasions to play for England as a striker. Rooney has played in the last two World Cups of 2006 and 2010. He was named the 2010 PFA Players' Player of the Year in April 2010.

Activity 4

1 Use Texts B and C for this activity.

2 Use the information you have read about Dimitar Berbatov and Wayne Rooney. Write a main point about both players. Start your sentence:

Berbatov and Rooney both...

3 Then add two details about each player to back up your main point.

Activity 5

1 Read Task A below.

> **Task A** Who is your hero? Write an article for your school website about a person you admire, explaining why you think they are a hero.

ResultsPlus
Watch out!

Your writing will be more convincing if you back up your main points with detailed evidence. Try to avoid repeating yourself – plan your answer so that each point leads on to the next.

2 Choose your hero. Here are some ideas:

Nelson Mandela   **firefighters**   **nurses**   **Wayne Rooney**
My grandad   **Anne Frank**

3 Think of at least two things you admire about your chosen hero. These will be your main points.

4 Now plan a paragraph for each of your main points. For each paragraph, plan to include:
- your main point
- evidence to support it, with details
- connectives to link your points.

For example:

Hero: Nelson Mandela

Paragraph	Main point	Evidence	Details
1	He fought apartheid in South Africa with great courage.	He spent 27 years in prison for what he believed in.	He believed in equal rights for black people. South Africa was ruled by white people. Black South Africans were not allowed to vote and had few rights.

5 Write a draft of one of your planned paragraphs.

6 Swap drafts with a partner. Discuss how well you have each included main points and details. Suggest ways in which the drafts could be improved.

Inverted commas

The details you use to back up a main point could include quotations. These are words that someone else has spoken or written. You should:

▶ Begin and end a quotation with inverted commas.

▶ Make the quotation part of your sentence. Introduce it with a comma.

▶ Make sure it is clear who is speaking.

For example:

> Nelson Mandela said, "There is no passion to be found playing small – in settling for a life that is less than the one you are capable of living."

Activity 6

1 Read the three quotations from famous people.

2 Write a sentence including each quotation. Make sure you use inverted commas correctly each time.

> If you can't feed a hundred people, then feed just one.

Mother Teresa, cared for the poor in Kolkata

> Music can change the world because it can change people.

Bono, musician and activist

> Focusing your life solely on making a buck shows a certain poverty of ambition. It asks too little of yourself.

Barack Obama, first black president of the USA

3 Go back to your draft paragraph that you wrote for Activity 5 opposite. Can you add extra detail to it by including a quotation?

8 Writing effective sentences

Always write in complete and correct sentences.

Simple sentences checklist

A simple sentence makes one point and has one verb. A verb is a word that shows an event or action taking place. The verbs in the following sentences have been highlighted for you:

The football players walked out of the tunnel.
I belong to a drama group.
My cat likes to sleep in the sunshine.

Before you write down a sentence, say it in your head. Ask yourself:

▶ Does it make sense?

▶ Has it got a verb?

▶ Is it clear who or what is doing the verb?

Then write your sentence down and check that it:

▶ Starts with a capital letter.

▶ Ends with a full stop, question mark or exclamation mark.

Activity 1

1 Read Text A opposite. It is an advert for a babysitting service.

2 Check each sentence in the text using the simple sentences checklist above.

3 Rewrite the text so that every sentence is correct and complete.

Text A

We offer a babysitting service.
Jas and Emily are both sensible and first aiders. Your child will enjoy our bedtime stories and calm approach Reasonable rates We can give you references from happy parents..

Activity 2

1 Read Text B. It is Ash's notes for an advert for his window-cleaning business.

2 Write Ash's leaflet in complete simple sentences.

Text B

very experienced
bring all my own equipment
let me do it rather than go up a ladder yourself
reasonable rates and a reliable service

Linking simple sentences

To make your writing flow well, you can link the points you are making into longer sentences. Use a connective. Some common connectives are:

and   or   but   because

▶ Use *and* or *because* to add another point that supports your first point, for example:

I want to go ice skating and I have my warm clothes.

▶ Use *or* to add an alternative to your first point, for example:

We could go ice skating or we could go for a coffee.

▶ Use *but* to add a point that disagrees with your first point, for example:

We could go ice skating but I would rather go for a coffee.

Activity 3

1 Read these simple sentences.
- I go fishing with my Uncle Sam.
- We get up really early.
- We take our breakfast with us.
- Sometimes it is not much fun.
- On a good day we catch some trout.
- I love bringing the catch home.
- My dad can cook them for tea.
- Sometimes we do not catch anything.

2 Use connectives to join some of these together to make three longer sentences. Think carefully about which connectives to use.

Vary your sentences

To make your writing more interesting, you can include:

▶ Statements, for example:
  'I want to go ice skating.' End statements with a full stop.

▶ Exclamations, for example:
  'I always fall over!' End exclamations with an exclamation mark.

▶ Questions, for example:
  'Have you got gloves?' End questions with a question mark.

Activity 4

1 Write an email to a friend, suggesting that you meet up this weekend. Include a statement, a question and an exclamation.

2 Swap emails with a partner and check each other's sentences.
  a Is every sentence complete and correctly punctuated?
  b Does the writing include a statement, a question and an exclamation?

ResultsPlus
Top tip

You can make your writing more interesting by linking simple sentences that are related with a suitable connective. Vary your writing by using different kinds of connectives.

Activity 5

1 Write a paragraph for a blog about what you enjoy doing in your spare time. Vary your sentences by using:
  • simple sentences
  • sentences linked together with connectives
  • statements, exclamations and questions.

2 Swap your paragraph with a partner. Check that they have used a variety of sentences, and that all sentences are correct and complete.

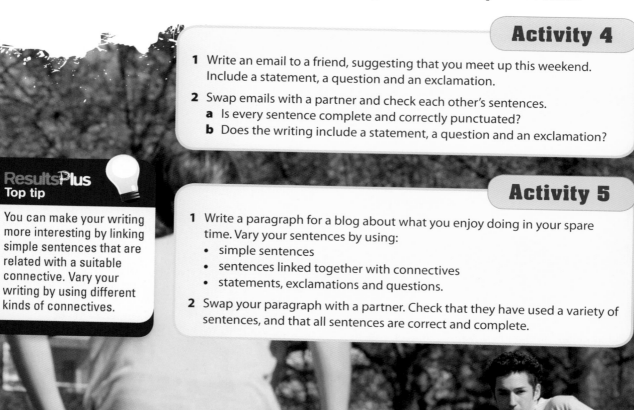

Punctuating sentences

Remember, your punctuation should help your reader to understand your meaning.

▶ Show that you are making a new point by starting a new sentence with a capital letter, for example:

He wants to learn to skate.

▶ Show that you have finished your point by ending your sentence with a full stop, question mark or exclamation mark, for example:

Do you want to learn to skate?

▶ Use commas to separate chunks of meaning, for example:

When you learn to skate you have to try your best, keep practising and always wear a helmet.

ResultsPlus
Top tip

Before you write down your sentence, decide how you will end it, then put in a full stop and start a new sentence. This will help you to avoid long, difficult-to-follow sentences with commas where full stops should be.

Activity 6

1 Read Text C below. It is a student's first draft of a text about a hobby. The text is difficult to follow because there is no punctuation.

2 Rewrite Text C, making it easier to follow by breaking it into correctly punctuated sentences.

Text C

one of my hobbies is keeping guinea pigs they are really sweet did you know that unlike rats they do not carry any nasty diseases they are also a lot easier to handle than a hamster guinea pigs get to know you and squeak happily when you bring them food you can teach them simple things like how to go through a maze if they find a treat each time they go along the right way I would really recommend keeping guinea pigs

Activity 7

1 Read Text D below.

2 Write a reply to the text, stating your own views. Vary your sentences and check that they are correct.

3 Swap your writing with a partner and check each other's work. Score one point for every correctly punctuated sentence. Score an extra point for each different type of sentence you use.

4 Give each other feedback and suggest ways to improve your sentences.

Text D

I think some breeds of dogs should be banned altogether, not just muzzled. In some countries the police destroy all dangerous dogs like pit bulls and they are dying out. They should do the same here because then there would be no more horrific incidents like children being mauled.

You may be asked to write an explanation or some instructions. This unit will help you to practise putting together the skills you have learned to write effectively.

This lesson will help you to:
▶ practise writing a complete text
▶ organise your points logically
▶ improve your spelling

Activity 1

1 Read Task A.

Task A

Imagine you volunteer at a community centre. You have been told that some of the older people who attend the centre would like to improve their technology skills.

Write a set of instructions for older people explaining how to use a computer to send an email.

2 Find the key words in the task that tell you the audience and purpose.

3 What form are you asked to write in?

4 What style would be appropriate for your instructions? Think about your purpose and audience to help you decide.

Gather your ideas

To write instructions, you need to:

▶ Picture yourself doing the activity one stage at a time.

▶ For each stage, make a brief note of what you need to tell your audience.

▶ Number the stages in the order in which they must be done.

For example, to write instructions on how to make a sandwich you might start like this:

> 1 Take two slices of bread.
> 2 Spread each slice with butter.

**ResultsPlus
Top tip**

Read your work back to yourself and check that you have included everything necessary to make your writing clear.

Activity 2

1 You are going to make a plan for Task A. Read the task again.

2 Picture yourself sending an email. For each stage of the process, make a brief note of what you need to write about.

3 Check that you have missed nothing out.

Form

Instructions are usually written as a series of points under a heading. Each point tells the reader what to do next.

The points may be numbered, for example:

How to make mashed potatoes

1 Peel four potatoes.
2 Cut them into cubes.

Or they could be linked together using time connectives, for example:

First peel four potatoes. Then cut them into cubes.

Some time connectives you could use are:

first next **then** **after that** **finally**

Practise using time connectives by working through Activity 3 below.

Activity 3

1 What is your favourite sandwich? Write a paragraph explaining how to make it. Use time connectives, for example:

First take a white roll. Then spread butter...

2 Swap your recipe with a partner. Take turns to act out making the sandwiches using the recipe.

3 Give your partner feedback on what was clear and what was confusing, for example, did they miss a step out? Were some details missing?

4 Re-draft your paragraph so that the instructions are completely clear.

Activity 4

1 Now go back to your plan for Task A, which you completed for Activity 2.

2 Decide whether you want to organise your points as a numbered list or in a paragraph with time connectives.

3 Add numbers or time connectives to your plan.

Using the right words

For your instructions or explanations to be clear, you must write accurately. Think about:

▶ The correct names for things, for example: *menu tab*.

▶ Verbs to describe actions, for example: *select* or *click*.

▶ Prepositions such as *above*, *under*, *on*, *below*, *beside*.

Practise using words accurately by working through Activity 5 below.

Activity 5

1 With a partner, take turns to give each other directions on how to walk from the entrance to your school to your classroom. Practise using:
  • the correct names for things, for example: *reception*
  • verbs, for example: *walk straight ahead*
  • prepositions, for example: *walk along the path beside the grass*.

2 Give each other feedback on how clear the directions were. What needs improving?

Activity 6

1 Now go back to your plan for Task A, which you worked on in Activities 2 and 4 on pages 94 and 95.

2 Write a first draft of your instructions. Remember to:
  • write appropriately for your audience and purpose
  • use the correct form
  • use time connectives or numbers to order your points
  • use accurate vocabulary.

3 Check your draft and make any improvements.

Improve your spelling

To be clear and effective, your writing must be accurate. Here are some students' ideas for ways to learn and remember spellings:

> I break words down into sounds: re-mem-ber.

> I use a rhyme or message: for 'necessary' I remember it has one collar (one 'c') and two sleeves (two 's's).

> I say it as it sounds: Wed-nes-day.

> I look words up in the dictionary.

> I use the spelling of a similar or rhyming word: l-ight and n-ight, for example.

> I look at a word, cover it, say it and then try to write it.

Activity 7

1 Think of three words that you find difficult to spell.

2 Choose one or more of the ideas above, or think of your own ideas, to help you spell them correctly.

Some words sound the same but are spelt differently and mean different things, for example:

there – to direct to a place	to – towards
their – to indicate ownership	two – more than one
they're – they are	too – as well

Activity 8

1 Read Ivan's first draft of some directions to a friend's party.

The party is on Wednsday. It's not diffcult to find. When you leave you're flat take the bus too the bus garaje. Their you'll need to catch the 49 and ask the driver to tell you wen your at Park Square. The flats are on the left and its number 6.

2 Find at least three spelling errors in Ivan's work.

3 Work out and write down the correct spellings. Use the students' strategies above to help you.

10 Practising writing clearly and logically (2)

You may be asked to write briefing notes. These summarise the main points of a meeting, event or task so that the reader is given all of the important information. This lesson will help you to practise putting together the skills you have learnt throughout the Writing section to write effectively.

To help your reader to understand your briefing notes, you need to:

▶ Plan a logical order for your information.

▶ Group ideas and information into different sections.

▶ Think of headings that sum up the main point of each section.

▶ Separate out different points within your sections, using bullet points and numbered lists.

Activity 1

1 Read Text A opposite.

2 a List the four main headings the writer uses in the text.
   b Match the descriptions below to these main headings.
      A Gives an overview of what is happening at the event.
      B Lists issues to be aware of.
      C Gives some background information on what the students have been investigating.
      D Provides information on what the reader can expect at the concert.
   c What other features are used to make the text easy to follow?

3 Record your answers in a table like the one below.

Main heading	What information is given	How this information is made easy to follow

Work Songs Concert at Didlock Community College

Introduction
GCSE and Diploma Music students have been investigating work songs. They will be explaining and performing ten work songs during the concert.

5 **Background**
- Work songs are sung by slaves, soldiers, prisoners, etc. while they work.
- They often have strong rhythms.
- The tunes are simple and easily remembered.
- Work songs help workers to overcome boredom when doing the same tasks all day long.

10 **Considerations**
- Students performing are aged 14 to 18.
- They come from different backgrounds.
- They have written new verses for some of the traditional songs.
- All achievements are being recognised.
15 - Some students have only just begun their courses.
- Many students may be extremely nervous.

At the concert
- Please arrive by 7pm at the main reception. You will be shown to your seat.
- Students will take turns to tell you about each song, including background information
20 and how and why the new version has been written, then each song will be performed.
- You can meet the students afterwards at an after-show party.

Activity 2

1 Read Task A below.

Task A

Imagine your local MP wants to find out more about education and is going to visit your school or college. Write a set of briefing notes for the MP so that they have information about your school or college and they are aware of what they should bear in mind during their visit.

2 a First, pick out the key words in the task that tell you:
- your audience
- your purpose
- the form you should write in.

b Keep referring back to these key words to make sure your writing stays focused.

3 Write down the headings below with space to write underneath them.
- Introduction
- Background
- Considerations
- During the visit

4 Now work out what information you could include under each heading. Think about:

Introduction: what the task tells you about the reason for the visit.

Background: information the MP might need about your school or college, the students they will meet and what lessons they will see.

Considerations: anything the MP should bear in mind during the visit, such as the ability levels and interests of the students.

During the visit: practical details of what will happen on the day.

5 Note down your ideas to make a plan for your writing.

6 Now draft your briefing notes. Use Text A on page 99 to help you. Make sure you:
- have a title summing up what the notes are for
- use all four headings
- organise your information under your headings, following your plan
- use a style that is appropriate for your audience
- present your information clearly – think about using bulleted lists or sub-headings.

7 Check your briefing notes carefully and correct any errors.

Verb tenses

A verb is a word that shows an event or action taking place, for example: *run, dance, write.*

To make your meaning clear for the reader, make sure you always use the correct tense. Tense refers to the time, such as whether an event happened in the past, is happening in the present or will happen in the future.

> **Past tense** – use this for events or actions that happened before now, for example:
> The class was large but some people left.
>
> **Present tense** – use this for events or actions that are happening now, for example:
> The class is quite small now.
>
> **Future tense** – use this for events or actions that have not happened yet, for example:
> The class will be bigger again next term.

Use the same tense to write about events or actions happening at the same time.

ResultsPlus
Top tip

If you can, leave some time to proofread your work carefully. Check that you have used the correct tense of verbs and that your punctuation and spelling are accurate. Use a dictionary if you are not sure of spellings.

Activity 3

1 Read Task A again on the opposite page.

2 Levine has written the background section of the briefing notes in the task. She needs to do more work on her verbs. Add verbs in the correct tense to each of the gaps in her work below.

> - There _____ now sixteen students in the English group. There _____ more but some left.
> - Students in the group also _____ a wide range of other courses.
> - When they leave, the students _____ all kinds of jobs.

3 Go back to the briefing notes you wrote for the task in Activity 2.
   a Underline the verbs in each sentence.
   b Check that they are in the right tense. Tick those that are right and circle any you think may be wrong.
   c Swap briefing notes with a partner. Check their marking of the verb tenses and discuss any tenses that you disagree about.
   d Rewrite any verbs that need correcting.

Writing mini-test – questions

On these pages you will find examples of the kinds of tasks you may encounter in your Writing test. For these practice tasks, you have been given some tips by the examiner. Use these to develop your skills – but remember, you won't be given these tips in the test.

Task 1

Information

You have to undertake a period of work experience as part of your studies. You have received the note below from the teacher who helps organise this.

Dear (**Your name**)

I have been sent details of some work placement opportunities at the Potter & Thomas Department store. The store has lots of different departments, including men's and women's clothing, health and beauty products, household
5 goods, electrical goods, sportswear, etc., so you might have a choice of departments to work in.

You will need to write a letter to the Human Resources Manager, Mrs Jill Walsh, applying for a two week placement in June. Don't forget to tell them about yourself and any work you have done in the past.

10 The address of Potter & Thomas is 26–30 Dunn Street, Bradfield, BD1 8LX.

Good luck!

Anna King

Anna King
Work Experience Co-ordinator

Writing task

Write a letter to Jill Walsh, the Human Resources Manager, asking for a placement for work experience at the store.

In your letter, you should:
· introduce yourself and your reason for writing
· explain the kind of work you would like to do
· describe your previous experience
· describe your personal qualities and interests.

Remember to set your letter out correctly.

(15 marks)

Task 2

Information

You have an unwanted gift for sale. Your local supermarket has a noticeboard where you can place a postcard free of charge to advertise the item you would like to sell.

Writing task

Write the text for an advert describing briefly and clearly what you want to sell.

In your advert, you may wish to include:
- a detailed description of the item
- your reason for selling
- the price you are asking for
- how buyers can contact you.

(10 marks)

On pages 104 to 109 you will find example 'pass' and 'fail' answers to the writing tasks on pages 102 to 103. Read the answers together with the examiner summaries to help you understand what is required to achieve a Level 1 pass.

Student 1: extracts typical of 'pass Level 1' answers

Question 1

15 Garden View

Barby

GY5 7FD

Mrs Jill Walsh
Human Resources Manager
26-30 Dunn Street
Bradfield
BF1 8LX

September 27th 2010

Dear Mrs Walsh,

My name is Aidan and I am a Year 10 pupil at Barby High School. I am writing to you to ask for two weeks of work experience at your store. I would like this in June because that is when we do our work experience at our school.

If you will let me I want to work in the sports department because I love sports and I am very intrested in that. In fact I am doing GCSE PE at school so I think it would be useful for me to have some experience about what things you sell.

I had a paper round for two years when I was younger and sometimes I help my dad in his shop so I am used to dealing with customers.

I am reliable and hard-working. I am hardly ever off school and never late. I have lots of freinds and get on well with people. As I said before, I am very keen on sports so I think I would be good in the Sports Department.

Please write back to me soon and tell me if you will let do my work experience at your store. Also which dates are avaliable. I am looking forward to hearing from you.

Yours sincerely

Aidan Jagger

Examiner summary

A: Form, communication and purpose = 8 marks
B: Spelling, punctuation and grammar = 5 marks
Total = 13/15

What has been done well?	
The answer fits the task	Clear explanation of the purpose of the letter and a good description of relevant personal qualities.
Appropriate tone for the purpose	Relatively formal, but since the audience is a specific person the direct address to the reader 'If you will let me…' is acceptable. The vocabulary is straightforward but appropriate for the purpose.
Correct letter format	Two addresses set out correctly, date, appropriate greeting and matching close.
Clear structure	Well-organised, using paragraphs for each section of the letter.
Accurate spelling	Only three spelling errors ('intrested', 'freinds' and 'avaliable').
Accurate punctuation	Full stops and occasional commas.
Grammatically correct	Accurate subject-verb agreement, use of tenses.

What could be improved?	
Include more detail about how this kind of work might be useful	For example, to gain new skills/confidence, to learn about the retail industry, to learn about a range of sportswear.
Provide alternatives to first choice	In case there are no vacancies in that department.
Include the name of the firm in the recipient's address	So it is easy to identify the correct organisation if the letter is delivered to the wrong address.
Vary the sentence structure	Use commas to separate units of meaning or use connectives to link ideas together. One sentence is incomplete: 'Also which dates are available.'

Student 1: extracts typical of 'pass Level 1' answers

Question 2

For Sale – Brand new, Italian Ice Skates. Never been woren. Pink with black lines on them and white laces. The skates are well padded with ankle support and has a Carbon steel blade. They are made by Roces. Size 5.

This gift is unwanted because I hurt my leg and cant skate. In the shops it costs £60 but I will sell for £45. If you are interested ring me on 0123 456789 any evening.

Examiner summary

A: Form, communication and purpose = 6 marks
B: Spelling, punctuation and grammar = 3 marks
Total – 9/10

What has been done well?	
Clear, concise description of item for sale, including relevant details	For example, make, size, colour, some design details, cost.
Logical organisation of information	Little or no unnecessary information presented mostly in a logical sequence.
Polite, business-like tone	Formal vocabulary, no use of slang.
Correct format	No need for complete sentences as long as the sense is clear.
Technically accurate	Few spelling mistakes. Accurate punctuation. Only minor grammatical slips: e.g 'The skates … has'.
Fluent, clear expression of ideas	Simple punctuation helps make meaning clear.

What could be improved?	
Occasional lapse in sequencing of ideas	For example, size and make could be described earlier to catch the reader's attention.
Use fewer words	For example, 'because I hurt my leg and cant skate' = 'owing to injury'.
Use capital letters only where necessary	'Ice Skates'; 'Carbon'.

Question 1

Paul Hill
112 gladstone rd
Newbridge
Ng4 1tL

Dear,
        jill
i am Paul Hill, i had to wright to you about if you can let me do Work experence in june. So
wot jobs had you got and the dates there avilabel becuase i can come enytime in june. i think
ther is lots of good jobs at yor stor for exampel you can sell cool cloths and maybe i can by
som cheep i wold relay like a Job so plees right back an tell me. thankyou
 from
Paul Hill

Examiner summary

A: Form, communication and purpose = 2 marks
B: Spelling, punctuation and grammar = 3 marks
Total – 5/15

What has been done well?	
Communicates main idea	Would like work experience in June.
Includes some features of correct layout	Own address in correct position, own name to close.

What could be improved?	
Include more personal information	For example, age, place of education, previous experience, personal qualities and interests.
Show understanding of purpose of work experience	For example, to develop skills, confidence, knowledge of industry.
Include name and address of person who should receive the letter	In a large company it may be misplaced after being opened.
Date the letter	Letters may be filed according to their date and you can use the date as a reference point if you need to write a follow-up letter.
Use appropriate greeting and close for a formal letter	Dear Mrs Walsh/Yours sincerely or Dear Madam/Yours faithfully.
Write in accurate sentences	Some sentences are too long with punctuation missing.
Use paragraphs	To group ideas together and help the reader to follow what you have written.
Technical accuracy	• Words which sound the same sometimes mean different things, for example wright/right/write, by/buy. • Common words which are often used, e.g. what, there, some. • End sentences with full stops not commas; use question marks for questions. • Subject-verb agreement, e.g. 'is lots of jobs'; use of correct tense, e.g. 'what jobs had you got'. • For example, the initial letter of names such as 'Gladstone Road', 'Jill','June' and first person pronoun 'I' but NOT for 'work' or 'job'.

Question 2

if u like a new fone ring 07219876543, I got it off my gran for my burthday but I alredy had a blackbery cerv and now Iv got 2 fones so Iam seling it cos its not as good but its still ok. It has a lot off assesorys such as camra and their are a radio an bluetoth and many more, alos a charjer but you dont realy need it cos its good on baterys. It is a nokia 2330

Examiner summary

A: Form, communication and purpose = 3 marks
B: Spelling, punctuation and grammar = 2 marks
Total – 5/10

What has been done well?	
Gives some relevant information	What is for sale, some features, contact details.

What could be improved?	
Present information in a logical sequence	Start by explaining the make and model of the item for sale.
Make sure you include all relevant information	For example, the price you would like.
Don't include unnecessary information	For example, 'I got it off my gran' and 'it's not as good' (as my other phone).
Avoid long rambling sentences	The sentence beginning 'I got it off my gran …' has several different ideas in it and would read better as two sentences, at least.
Technical accuracy	Spelling errors include: • Common words (and, also, really, birthday) • Words with different meanings that sound the same (of/off, there/their) • Technical words (phone, camera, Bluetooth) • Plurals of words ending in 'y' (accessories, batteries) Punctuation errors include: • Missing full stops (last sentence) • Commas instead of full stops (e.g first line) • Missing apostrophes (it's, don't) Grammatical errors include: • Incorrect tense (like/would like) • Lack of subject-verb agreement (there are a radio) • Failing to use capital letters to begin a sentence ('if u like…') or for brand names (Blackberry, Nokia)

Introduction to Functional Skills English Assessment

This section of the book will help you to prepare for your Functional Skills English Level 1 assessment.

Understand how you will be assessed

You will be assessed for your skills in:

▶ Reading

▶ Speaking, listening and communication

▶ Writing

On the following pages you will find a description of exactly how you will be assessed for each area. You are also given a list of top tips from the examiner. These tips are based on the examiner's experience of marking Functional Skills English assessments. Use them to prepare in order to make sure you secure every mark that you can.

Practice assessments

You will then be given practice exams and assessments:

▶ Pages 118 to 123 – practice Reading paper

▶ Pages 124 to 125 – practice Speaking, Listening and Communication assessment tasks

▶ Pages 126 to 127 – practice Writing paper

ResultsPlus
Self-assessment

When you have completed the assessments, review your work with a partner or with your teacher. Look at the 'Top tips for success' on pages 115–117. What areas of your work are you confident in and what needs further improvement? Record your self-assessment and set a plan for any areas you need to work on.

Reading

Your reading is assessed in one 45-minute exam. The total number of marks for the reading paper is 20.

The reading paper is divided into two sections: A and B. Each section has a text to read and questions to answer about it. Each question states the number of marks it is worth. The two texts are on the same subject or theme. You will be given space to write your answers.

The table below shows the types of question you will be asked and what you should do in each case.

Types of question	What you should do
Multiple choice	Select the correct option to complete an unfinished sentence or to answer a question. Put a cross in a box to show your answer
Find a number of pieces of information and evidence in the text	Give short written answers
Identify features of the text that tell you what kind of text it is	Give a short written answer **or** select several options from a list, putting a cross in a box to show your answer
Respond to the text by using information in it	Write a short answer based on information from the text. There will be a number of possible answers

Speaking, listening and communication

Your speaking, listening and communication skills will be assessed by your teacher. You may take time ahead of your assessments to research and prepare what you want to say, and you can use notes to help you on the day.

The table below shows the tasks you will have to complete and what you should do in each case. Your two discussions should have different contexts and subjects, including some unfamiliar subjects.

Type of task	Who with?	Time	You must show that you can
Formal discussion	About four others	About 15 minutes	Make relevant and extended contributions to discussions Allow for and respond to others' input Prepare for and contribute to discussions of ideas and opinions
Informal discussion	Up to four others	About 15 minutes	Make different kinds of contributions Present information and points of view clearly Use appropriate language

Your writing is assessed in one 45-minute exam. There are two tasks that assess your writing skills. The total number of marks for the Writing paper is 25: 15 marks for task 1 and 10 marks for task 2.

For each task, you will be given some information. You will then be given a writing task based on it. You will be told what form to write in and given some guidance on what to include.

The table below shows what you will be assessed on and what you should do in each case.

What you will be assessed on	You must show that you can
Form, communication and purpose	Use the correct format for your writing, such as a correctly laid-out letter
	Organise your writing logically
	Communicate effectively the information the reader needs
	Use appropriate language for the purpose
	Write to meet the purpose, such as to inform
Spelling, punctuation and grammar	Ensure your spelling and grammar are generally accurate and the reader can understand your meaning
	Use a range of punctuation generally correctly

Reading

- Make sure you answer all the questions – keep an eye on the time.

- Check the marks for the question and the space given for your answer. These will give you clues about how much to write.

- Read each question carefully before you look for the answer. Look for key words in the question to help you focus.

- Read the texts carefully, using all your reading skills.

- Only include information taken from the right text. You will gain no marks for information from other sources.

- For multiple choice, more than one answer may be **almost** right – read carefully to choose the one that is **exactly** right.

- Use your own words in your answers.

- Remember, you are allowed to use a dictionary. If there is a word you don't understand, check if it is explained for you. Look it up if you need to.

- Check your answers at the end if you have time.

Speaking, listening and communication

- Prepare by researching the subject and deciding what points you want to make.

- Be clear about your purpose and focus on achieving it.

- Be clear about your point of view and what you want to get across.

- Be clear about your audience and situation. Adjust your language to make sure it is suitable.

- Make brief notes to help you stay on track.

- Speak calmly and slowly, and not too loudly or quietly. Make sure everyone can hear you.

- Make eye contact with your audience.

- When others speak, listen carefully, respond politely and treat everyone's ideas as worth considering.

- Make sure you answer both questions — keep an eye on the time.

- Read the information you are given carefully.

- Read the task closely. Make sure you are clear about what writing form to use, such as an email or a letter.

- Show that you know and understand the features of the text you are asked to write.

- Write down your purpose for writing and your audience. Suit your writing to them.

- Make a quick plan to help you organise your ideas and plan paragraphs. Plan to back up your points with evidence.

- Don't waste time laying out your writing in columns or including drawings — you will not get marks for this.

- Use a range of different sentence types and connectives to link sentences.

- Check your spelling, punctuation and grammar carefully. Use a dictionary if necessary. You will lose marks for mistakes.

- Try to allow time to check your writing at the end. Correct any mistakes and make any improvements that you can.

Section A

Read Text A and answer questions 1–7.

You are interested in reality TV shows. You have found this web page on the internet.

Text A

In the Spotlight – TV Talent Shows

TV 'talent' shows never fail to attract viewers. The chance to see fresh new talent combined with hilariously terrible performances prove far too entertaining for the majority of the general public to resist.

For the lucky few, reality TV is a quick launch into stardom, as proven by the success of X-Factor stars Leona Lewis and JLS. Yet for the 'wannabe' hopefuls who *think* they're the next Beyoncé or Robbie (but in reality sound more like a tone-deaf strangled cat), a few painful seconds in the spotlight only ends in public humiliation and defeat.

So what makes people apply for these shows without really knowing whether it will lead to success or failure? Here are some of the pros and cons – you have been warned...!

Pros

- Exposure – the opportunity to perform in front of celebrity judges, a live TV audience and millions of TV viewers.
- Media – free publicity from newspapers, magazines and radio stations, though beware of negative publicity as well as positive!
- Experience – the chance to visit a television studio and see how the programme is recorded.
- Prizes – you could be offered a recording and management contract, even if you don't win the show.

Cons

- Queues – enjoy queuing at your local supermarket/bus stop? Well, you can expect to queue for several hours before even getting to the sign-in desk to register!
- Auditions – contestants are usually screened by the show's producer or a representative from the management company and may not even meet the celebrity judges at all.
- Performance – we've all seen how Simon Cowell treats the contestants, so be prepared for criticism!
- Cameras – the contestant must be prepared to be filmed during the whole process, so give up now if you're camera-shy.

Answer questions 1 to 3 with a cross in the box [☒]. If you change your mind about an answer, put a line through the box [☒] and then mark your new answer with a cross [☒].

1 The main purpose of this web page is:

☐	A	To instruct you how to apply for an audition
☐	B	To warn you against watching TV talent shows
☐	C	To persuade you to audition for a TV talent show
☐	D	To inform you of issues affecting TV talent show applicants

(1 mark)

2 According to the web page, one advantage of appearing in a TV talent show is:

☐	A	you will be auditioned by celebrity judges
☐	B	you may be filmed at any time
☐	C	you will see how the programme is made
☐	D	you will win a prize

(1 mark)

3 A feature of Text A that shows it is a web page is:

☐	A	menu
☐	B	sub-headings
☐	C	bold text
☐	D	bullet points

(1 mark)

4 Name **one** reason reality TV shows are popular with television companies.

....

(1 mark)

5 List **two** reasons given in Text A why audiences enjoy reality TV shows.

You do **not** need to write in sentences.

i) ....

ii) ....

(2 marks)

6 List **two** important personal qualities suggested by the text for someone wanting to apply to appear on a TV talent or reality show.

You do **not** need to write in sentences.

i) ....

....

ii) ....

....

(2 marks)

7 What advice would you offer to someone going to an audition for a TV talent show?

Give **two** suggestions using the information from Text A.

You do **not** need to write in sentences.

i) ....

....

ii) ....

....

(2 marks)

TOTAL FOR SECTION A = 10 MARKS

Section B

Read Text B and answer questions 8–13.

You have found this advertisement on a website.

Dream School – New show with Jamie Oliver

What's wrong with school?

Have you left school knowing you could do better?
Are you dyslexic?
5 Are you are a teenage mum?
Were you bullied?
Have your parents paid for your education but you have still not fulfilled
your potential?

If any of this sounds like you, we want to hear from you!

10 Jamie Oliver and Fresh One Productions are setting up a school... but with
a difference.

We are looking for 16–19-year-olds to take part in a new documentary
series for Channel 4 this summer. If you would like more details, or know
someone who you think would be perfect, please apply today! Greater
15 London applicants only please.

Any personal details you give us will be kept securely and only used for the
purpose of considering your potential involvement in the programme. If you
are under 18, please check your parent/guardian is happy for you to speak
to us before calling.

- -

20 **Category:**   Reality/Documentary
    Applications Close: 15th July
    Filming in: London
    Applicants from: Greater London

Apply through the website - FREE
Write your application and send it directly to the show's research team
(Apply now)

Apply by video - FREE
Send a video audition straight to the show's research team
(Apply now)

Answer question 8 with a cross in the box you think is correct (☒). If you change your mind about an answer, put a line through the box (☒) and then mark your new answer with a cross (☒).

8 What is the **main** purpose of this web page?

☐	A	To inform you about a new reality TV show
☐	B	To advertise a new school
☐	C	To persuade you to apply as a contestant
☐	D	To advise you on educational problems

(1 mark)

Answer question 9 with a cross in the two boxes you think are correct (☒). If you change your mind about an answer, put a line through the box (☒) and then mark your new answer with a cross (☒).

9 Identify **two** features from the list below that show Text B is an advertisement.

☐	A	Paragraphs
☐	B	Sub-headings
☐	C	Links to 'apply now'
☐	D	Address and date
☐	E	Numbered list
☐	F	Use of questions

(2 marks)

10 Your friend wants to make an application, but is concerned about sending in personal details.

Using Text B give **two** reasons to reassure your friend about privacy.

You do **not** need to write in sentences.

i) ....

....

ii) ....

....

(2 marks)

11 Identify **two** details which are essential for anyone who applies for Dream School.

You do **not** need to write in sentences.

i) ....

ii) ....

(2 marks)

12 According to Text B, what should you do before applying if you are under 18?

You do **not** need to write in sentences.

....

(1 mark)

13 You would like to recommend someone for Dream School.

Using the information from Text B, identify **two** types of educational problems you would consider when choosing who might be suitable.

You do **not** need to write in sentences.

i) ....

....

ii) ....

....

(2 marks)

TOTAL FOR SECTION B = 10 MARKS

TOTAL FOR PAPER = 20 MARKS

Informal discussion

As part of its anti-bullying policy, your school or college is keen to encourage people to think for themselves. You have been asked to discuss your ideas for dealing with peer pressure.

In pairs or small groups, discuss how peer pressure can affect you.

Remember that people hold informal discussions all the time, and often there is no time to prepare your ideas beforehand. If possible, make some quick notes listing points you could make in the discussion. Some ideas to get you started are given below.

I don't like being the odd one out! People might laugh at me if I do things differently to everyone else.

I don't want to be like everybody else. People respect you for having your own ideas.

If all my friends are doing something I don't want to be left out.

Why should I always have to go along with everyone else? What about what I want to do?

Some people would rather get into trouble than lose their friends.

A good friend is someone who backs you up when you want to go against the group.

It's good to share things in common with other people but you don't always have to be the same.

Formal discussion

Your school or college canteen is reviewing its menus. The Canteen Manager has asked for input from pupils about what they would like to see on the menu to make school meals healthier and more interesting.

In a group of up to five, put forward your suggestions and discuss them. Your aim is to produce a list of four or five realistic proposals that the majority of the group can agree on.

Prepare for the discussion by writing down some ideas and researching information you think you might need so that you can speak with confidence and authority. Some ideas to get you started are given below.

School cooks and caterers have to follow Government guidelines about what school meals contain. For example:

- deep-fried foods such as battered fish cannot be served more than twice a week
- starchy foods cooked in fat or oil (e.g. chips, roast potatoes, Yorkshire pudding, etc.) cannot be offered more than three times a week
- an average secondary school lunch must contain a minimum of 5.2 grams of dietary fibre (from foods such as brown rice, wholemeal pasta, potatoes with skins, etc.)

By the year 2020, it's estimated that 30% of boys and 40% of girls will be obese.

Fizzy drinks cause tooth decay which affects about half of 15-year-olds.

Why do some people prefer to bring a packed lunch or go out of school at lunchtime? What might persuade them to try school lunches?

How much are people prepared to pay for a school lunch? Are healthy foods more expensive?

Is there enough variety of food on offer? Is there something to suit all the different cultures represented in the school?

The menus are always the same old thing – what about trying something a bit different? But there is a risk that no-one will buy it and lots of food will be wasted.

There are **two** tasks which assess your writing skills. Task 1 is worth 15 marks and Task 2 is worth 10 marks.

Remember that spelling, punctuation and grammar will be assessed in **both** tasks.

You may use a dictionary.

Task 1

Information

With a group of friends, you have organised a sponsored car wash to raise money for the Children In Need Appeal. Sponsors can buy tickets to have a car washed or pledge to pay a fee based on the number of cars washed on the day. You have volunteered to write a leaflet which can be handed out to advertise the event.

Writing task

Write an advertising leaflet for the sponsored car wash.

In your leaflet, you should include:

- the date, time and place of the sponsored car wash
- why you have organised the event and what you hope to achieve
- how much you will charge and how people can pay
- any other details you feel are important.

TOTAL FOR TASK 1 = 15 MARKS

Task 2

Information

You have arranged to hold your sponsored car wash in your school or college car park. The caretaker, Alan Booth, has asked you to email him with details of what you require.

Writing task

Write an email to Alan Booth with your requests for the car wash.

In your email, you may wish to:

- state the date of the car wash and the times you need the car park to be opened and closed
- check details of how to access the water supply
- state whether you are bringing your own equipment (buckets, mops, cloths, hosepipes, etc) or asking to borrow them from the school or college
- include any other details you feel are important.

TOTAL FOR TASK 2 = 10 MARKS

TOTAL FOR PAPER = 25 MARKS